I0816424

I'M AN ARCHITECT

ALFONSO FEMIA

ARCHITECTURE
AND GENEROSITY
BY PAUL ARDENNE

Marsilio

ARCHITECTURE,
BEFORE BEAUTY,
BEFORE AESTHETICS,
BEFORE SPACE,
IS THE ENCOUNTER
BETWEEN THE IMAGINARY
AND THE REAL

TO MARIANNA.

ENCHANTING THE WORLD

INTRODUCTION BY MAURICE CULOT

— *Apollinaire was just 18 years old when he wrote* L'Enchanteur pourrissant (The Rotting Magician) *in 1899. Embellished with wood-cut engravings by André Derain, this somewhat theatrical and poetic narrative was first published in 1909.*

— *The text translates the poet's quest for identity through the figure of Merlin, the son of a demon and a mortal. Despite his wisdom and self-knowledge, the magician, like the prophet, the poet and the artist, is a solitary being.*

He has the painful gift of being able to see that which cannot be seen by others. Merlin reveals his visions and secrets to the beautiful Viviane who turns them against him, less out a desire for a female vengeance over men than by the desperation of not being able to share with him. This leads Merlin, on his deathbed, to receive tributes from all the magical, bewitching, charming and demonic fauna and all the personas from the founding narratives to be found in Greek, Hebrew and Christian texts.

They all participate in the development of the poet's myth. From the Latin 'incantare' meaning enchantment or the Old French word 'ensorcerer' (meaning 'bewitching') and derived from 'sorcerer', it is always the incantatory voice that can be heard, the one that calls on imagination and gives birth to immediate effects and that cannot be controlled by calculation. Conversely, disenchantment is the dissolution of this world with its impregnation of myths and culture.

— *I look at the work produced by Alfonso Femia – the projects and constructions as well as the writings that he produces with his workshops or that he inspires in those around him – and the myth of the Magician immediately springs to mind. Given the increasingly inhospitable shores of reality as well as the ever-more difficult task o f attaining a shared urbanity, architects and builders might well find themselves tempted to just give up or go against the stream.*

The break with the past, the process of rationalisation resulting from the globalisation of the economy, society's massification and fragmentation, the development of communications and the flow of information, the increasing ignorance of decision-makers, the growing authority of standards and the increasing influence

of moralism result in men and women who are inclined towards interiority and spirituality finding themselves increasingly dispossessed.
The idea of the gay progress that accompanied my childhood is now obsolete.
As remarked by the French president Jacques Chirac in one of his most notable speeches given on the 2nd of September 2002 during the 4th Earth Summit held in Johannesburg: "Our house is burning down".

__ The injunction to act to stop the world from hardening and shrivelling is not easy for anybody, let alone for architects, as all constructions, if one were to refer to international standards, participate in the world's entropy. The construction of wooden buildings, the increasing use of electric cars, the community's participation in urban projects and other ancillary measures are, as we all know, no more than window-dressing, fig-leafs increasingly based on ecological blackmail.
The forest of obstacles has become so impenetrable that Léon Krier, the great theorist of the New Urbanism, even goes as far as to say: "I am an architect because I do not build".

__ Independently from the results, whose appreciation is based on individual tastes, Alfonso Femia has chosen to confront this aporia. His experience, right up to the limits of what is possible, has led him to develop an open and generous approach based on a genius loci *that distances itself from the dictatorship of fashion. All his projects incorporate the works of craftsmen and women and artists as active partners in the design process.*
It is an approach that goes far beyond the masquerade of the 1% cultural contribution that has prevailed for so long in France.
It was this close association between architecture and the applied arts that in the past led to the development of the Art Nouveau and Art Deco movements that were born in France and which subsequently spread across the world. In Italy, it is a shared if not genetic character trait that, without any excessive soul-searching, it is able to accommodate the buildings constructed by previous and successive generations.
It is a type of ambient magical realism particularly well illustrated

by Federico Fellini who, in his film Roma, *confronts the day-to-day lives of those living in the Eternal City and their reaction to the brutal intrusion of massive infrastructure works.*

— The idea of matter, in other words that from which we were banished 15 billion years ago, is essential in the ideas developed by Alfonso Femia. Whether for the ice factory in Milan, the Docks in Marseille, the Arches in Algiers or the housing in Asnières-sur-Seine, the materials and how they are used act as a hand outstretched to all, creating a local friendly relationship, a deliciously nostalgic complicity. He has chosen to place emphasis on dialogue and to play with materials.

This participative approach towards the 'all' is reminiscent of the Correspondances *by Baudelaire which, through the power of poetry, seeks to pick out the analogies that exist between the material world and the spiritual world.*

— Thus armed, Alfonso does not need to imagine architecture in terms of an affirmation of a personal style or in terms of positioning with regards other architects or critical evaluation.

— It seems to me that he sees his profession as a constantly renewed quest that seeks to develop constructive but often complicated relations with third parties. He does this within the framework of day-to-day relationships with non-idealised men and women - relationships within which imagination plays an important role.

As can be seen, it is not a question of populist participation, an easy escape route from professional and political responsibilities, but rather a way of thinking architecture that incorporates generosity and that takes care not to overcome or denigrate others. He reveals that talent does not require arrogance to impose itself. In a society as complicated as ours, dialogue among equals contributes more to the architecture than governmental measures even though one does have to admit that the latter have in the past resulted in the production of a large number of marvels. It goes without saying that within his workshops, he fully applies the principles of friendship and local specificity to urbanism. He now finds himself in a position opposite that of the idea that, although generous, provides undifferentiated and socially flattening solutions in the form of large homogenous blocks and urbicidal masterplans *that are both conceptual and abstract.*

__ It is a way of thinking that is difficult to summarise in just a few words or through a slogan. Antoine Pompe, an important name in Belgian architecture, when confronted with the functionalism of Le Corbusier and his emulators, proposed the alternative of an architecture based on Reason and Feeling.

What do you think, Alfonso?

Dear Maurice,

__ I believe that the project is the encounter between two spirits: that of the setting and that of humanity. Architecture is not an act of service, but rather one of feeling. If we were to lose this unique force that each of us carries within ourselves, then we would lose the place held by humanity over Time.
__ Since the creation of the agency, I have continued to develop the concept of a 'visionary pragmatism' that allows me to imagine architecture as lying at the heart of a founding imaginative realism created by humanity and for humanity.
__ Architecture must express reality and, to achieve that, we need to have both reason and feeling. Leonardo da Vinci expressed it this way: "Ogni nostra cognizione, principia da' sentimenti".
I strongly believe in this value that represents the magic of life and humanity. We are Time and we cross through with our thoughts and feelings. The most difficult part is to achieve this with sincerity and generosity as, without these aspects, we are incapable of living the magic of the world and humanity. We would be nothing but solitude.

The South will always be present to teach this to us.

And we all have a South accompanying us.

THE GARDENS OF GABRIEL
2013 – 2016
Asnières-sur-Seine, France
10,500 sqm

REDEVELOPMENT OF THE MARKET HALL
2017
Aosta, Italy
3,500 sqm

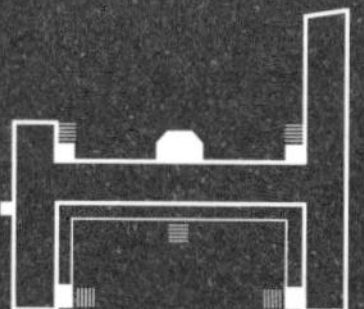

VILLA SUPRAMUROS
2018 – ongoing
Avignon, France
7,540 sqm

REDEVELOPMENT OF VILLA BORROMEO D'ADDA
2014 – 2018
Arcore, Italy
3,500 sqm

LIFE. NEW RESIDENTIAL DISTRICT
2010 – 2013
Brescia, Italy
26,492 sqm

TOURISTIC COMPLEX
2016 – ongoing
La Ciotat, France
16,115 sqm

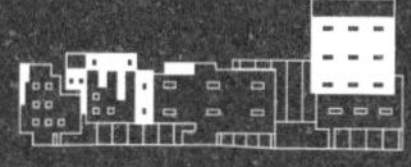

CONNECTED PROJECT OF GRAND PARIS EXPRESS
2015 – ongoing
Créteil-l'Échat, France
22,000 sqm

PROGRAMMING AND URBAN STUDY
2011
Grand Paris, France
211,000 sqm

SAN GIOVANNI EXHIBITION CENTRE
2002 – 2008
Casarza Ligure, Italy
250 sqm

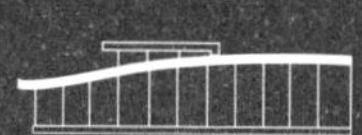

EUROPACITY: AFFORDABLE CHIC HOTEL 3*
2017 – ongoing
Gonesse, France
20,924 sqm

THREE TOWERS IN SAN BENIGNO
2010 – 2015
Genoa, Italy
25,346 sqm

IULM 6 UNIVERSITY
2003 – 2015
Milan, Italy
19,753 sqm

PIETRO MARIO BEGHI CIVIC LIBRARY
2012 – 2016
La Spezia, Italy
4,500 sqm

NEW CRUISE TERMINAL
2019 – ongoing
La Spezia, Italy
31,300 sqm

THE MARSEILLES DOCKS
2009 – 2015
Marseille, France
21,000 sqm

BÌ – TOY AND ARTS FACTORY
2005 – 2010
Cormano, Italy
2,000 sqm

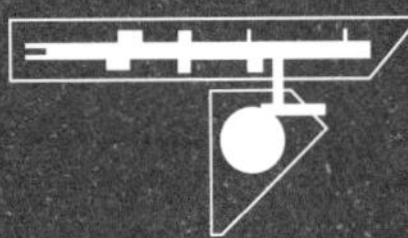

J1 THE ODYSSEY, SUBAQUATIC CITY
2018
Marseille, France
46,611 sqm

HORIZONTAL TOWER
2008 – 2010
Milan, Italy
25,730 sqm

LIBRARY, GAMEROOM AND AUDITORIUM
2002 – 2008
Casarza Ligure, Italy
582 sqm

NEW SCHOOL COMPLEX
2010 – 2013
Zugliano, Italy
3,500 sqm

THE VAULTS OF ALGIERS
2018 – ongoing
Algiers, Algeria
25,500 sqm

BNL-BNP PARIBAS HEADQUARTERS
2012 – 2016
Rome, Italy
75,000 sqm

EAI SITE, MONTPELLIER
2018
Montpellier, France
28,446 sqm

MC2 CREATIVITY CENTER
2018 – ongoing
Marseille, France
3,454 sqm

NEW VIMAR LOGISTICS POLE
2015 – ongoing
Marostica, Italy
52,612 sqm

THE CORNER
2014 – 2019
Milan, Italy
18,000 sqm

DALLARA ACADEMY
2015 – 2018
Varano de' Melegari, Italy
5,300 sqm

MILANESE ICE FACTORY
2002 – 2008
Milan, Italy
27,480 sqm

POSTE BRUNE XIV
2014 – 2017
Paris, France
18,000 sqm

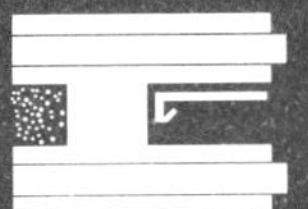

GREAT RAILWAYS WORKSHOPS
2009 – 2011
Turin, Italy
24,500 sqm

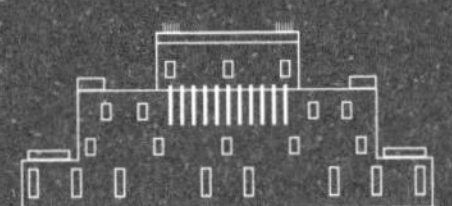

REDEVELOPMENT OF THE 1ST ITALIAN STATE MINT
2019
Rome, Italy
11,300 sqm

ITALIAN SPACE AGENCY
2005 – 2012
Rome, Italy
28,600 sqm

LES DOCKS DE MARSEILLE CORPS, SENTIMENTS ET MERVEILLE. CHAQUE
DES BÂTIMENTS QUI PEUVENT ÊTRE QUALIFIÉS D'HÉROÏQUES ET QUI SE
PÉRENNITÉ. DÉFINIS PAR LEURS DIMENSIONS PHYSIQUES ET LEUR
UNE GRANDE PARTIE D'ENTRE EUX A ÉTÉ CONSTRUITE À DES ÉPOQUES
PENSÉS COMME DES «MACHINES», DES OBJETS OU ENCORE DES
CES BÂTIMENTS PERSISTENT À NOS CÔTÉS ET SONT AUTANT DE
CETTE DIMENSION QUE NOUS APPELONS «HÉROÏQUE» EST RARE ET
DE BÂTIMENTS SAVENT CONCILIER LES CONTRASTES QUI PEUVENT
LEUR ÂME. NOUS SOMMES PARTIS À LA RECHERCHE DU CORPS ET DE L'ÂME
ET AVONS TENTÉ DE RENFORCER LE DIALOGUE LES LIANT L'UN À L'AUTRE.
COMME ON S'APPROCHE D'UNE ÉNIGME, COMME ON DÉCOUVRE UN
ÉTÉ TOUJOURS PRÉSENT DANS LA VILLE, CET ÉDIFICE NÉCESSITAIT
CONFRONTÉE À D'AUTRES NATURES, D'AUTRES RELATIONS, D'AUTRES INTIMITÉS
AUJOURD'HUI, LE BÂTIMENT SE VIT AVANT TOUT COMME UNE LIMITE
L'OUEST, ENTRE LA NOUVELLE VILLE CONTEMPORAINE ET LA MER,
ET LE SUD, ENTRE LA VILLE DE DEMAIN ET LE CENTRE HISTORIQUE
ET SOCIAL, LES DOCKS DE MARSEILLE DOIVENT ASSUMER LE RÔLE DE
PAR LE CONTEXTE. LIEU DE RENCONTRE PAR EXCELLENCE, CE BÂTIMENT
LES EXPRESSIONS DIVERSES D'UNE VILLE MÉDITERRANÉENNE QUI,
AVONS TOUT D'ABORD TRAITÉ DES QUESTIONS CONCERNANT LE
DEVENIR LE BÂTIMENT DES DOCKS, EN RAPPORT À CE QU'IL A ÉTÉ,
PERSONNEL ET INTIME, PRODUCTIF ET SOCIAL. CETTE TRANSFORMATION
À CONDITION D'UNE INTERVENTION CONTINUE ET VOLONTAIRE. LE
SON CORPS, UNE MASSE UNITAIRE ET CONTINUE. EN DEVENANT
PERCEPTIF DU BÂTIMENT AVEC L'EXTÉRIEUR EST RENFORCÉ. IL EST ALORS

LES DOCKS

VEHICLE DYNAMICS
INNOVATION
MOTOR VALLEY
AERODINAMICA

Bì

FILASTROCCA DI
FILASTROCCA
FAMMI
UN GENNAIO COL SO
UN LUGLIO FRE
MARZO GENTILE VOG
GIORNO SENZA SERA
UN MARE SENZA
UN PANE SEMP
SUL CIPRESSO
DEL PESCO CHE SIANO
GATTO E IL CANE
LE FONTANE
NON DARMI
UNA FACCIA
SOLAMENTE / ALLA
CHIEDO SCUSA ALLA
ANTICA SE NON MI
AVARA FORMICA
PARTE DELLA CICA
IL PIU BEL CANTO NON
REGALA / I BRAVI
UN SIGNORE DI SCAN
BUTTAVA LE CASTAGNE
GIAVA I RICCI UN SUO
DI LASTRA A SIGNA
PER FARE IL FRU
VUOLE IL FIORE
FARE UN TAVOLO
FIUMI NON
PONTI NON
SENTIERI
SUI MONTI
SCARPE NE
NON TROVAVI
OCCHIALI PER FA
UNA PARTITA NON
PALLONI
IL FUOCO PER

MC²
MC

to be continued...

CONTINUING THE STORY

— Whether they concern global demographic growth, rural exodus, gentrification, urban spread or lack of housing, these known data place considerable negative pressure on architecture. The need to build rapidly, on a large scale and at a low cost has the effect of sanctifying a homogenised and anonymous 'cut and paste' type of architecture while the construction of quality buildings finds itself reduced to extravagant projects.
The exceptional sculptural opera house or the inimitable look of an architect-designed home are no more than the attractive trees that have difficulty in hiding away a growing forest of *urbi et orbi* urban developments on the outskirts of towns.
It has already been quite some time since the Californian valleys that in the past had acted as green barriers between constructed entities have been moth-eaten by dull suburbanisation and that Moscow, London and Tokyo have battled it out to see who would hold first place on the podium for the endless city award, a concept lauded by the Spanish architect Arturo Soria but that was also seen as being grim, insipid and 'without qualities' to quote the unflattering formula used by the writer Robert Musil [1]. Acting within this context as an architect and urban planner and to refuse easy solutions is far from being a simple task and can even sometimes be compared to a 'combat sport' battled out against the 'granite blocks' represented by the need, urgency and dominant influence resulting from tight budgets.
Promoting a better architecture? It is nevertheless here, despite the hurdles, that Atelier(s) Alfonso Femia resolved to fight its battle and also chose its battlefront name of AF517 – the whale

[1] Robert Musil, "The Man Without Qualities", London, Martin Secker & Warburg, 1953 1954-1960

and its star – three architectural agencies forming a single entity, run by Alfonso Femia and with offices in Genoa, Milan and Paris.

__ Fight to produce the best, despite complicating circumstances. Accommodate with the aim of giving more by placing imagination at the service of the project.

— As a Mediterranean and European entity, Atelier(s) Alfonso Femia is fed by the fertile spirit represented by the *mare nostrum* and Paris, the City of Lights, while also adhering to the European values of progress, humanism and human rights. Lying between contextualisation and an open approach, the agency's 'ethic' is based on three pillars: adaptability, a greater offer and the development of an imaginative approach.

An Italian born in Calabria, Alfonso Femia began his career as an architect and urban planner in Genoa in the early 1990s. In 1995, he created the 5+1 agency in the Ligurian capital which, ten years later, became 5+1AA. The agency's capacities soon found themselves reaching out to Milan and then Paris.

In July 2017, the architect redefined, on the basis of his first foundations, the agency in "Atelier(s) Alfonso Femia / AF517", an agency that is now firmly established in three locations: Genoa, Milan and Paris.

This reveals the continuity of his professional trajectory, his choices and his idea of a journey within the journey.

What meaning could be given to the name AF517?

In 2017, Alfonso Femia turned 51. As well as being accustomed to return trips between Milan and Paris, he was also used to Air France flight numbers linking Genoa to Charles de Gaulle airport in Paris. Placed behind the architect's initials (A. F.), the number chosen to designate the agency is also the identifier for a submarine, a metaphor highly attractive to Alfonso Femia who is fascinated by the world of underwater research carried out far, far away from surface noises. He also likes odd numbers. As an agency expressing continuity and renewal, Atelier(s) Femia / AF517 extends the spirit of 5+1AA. The result is an adapted architecture, one that respects the client, is contextual and dialogues with the environment. It is an architecture able to enhance the delicate relations with a user that must always be pampered. These are fundamental principles that Alfonso Femia considers vital and represent the foundations underlying his approach. The mainspring for the new structure, with its acronym laden with an imaginative approach, is to push things even further along. Continuing the adventure implies being future-oriented and radicalising positions already held. Showing an awareness of what already exists (that which is already there) and the *genius loci* [2] (what the setting already has in terms of heritage) are two AF517 positions equivalent to a signature but which in noway prevent more open approaches, no matter whether the architectural project is intimate, social or even dreamt, with the whole backed by a utopian spirit.

[2] Christian Norberg-Schulz, "Genius Loci", New York, Rizzoli, 1980

It is the result of acquired experience.

__ Taking a realistic attitude on the one hand and incorporating local historicity on the other, alongside the integration of affects and the fantastic nourish the setting where the architect operates and contributes to the creation of an environment.

This has led to a triple methodological inflexion that had already germinated with 5+1AA and become increasingly refined with the Atelier(s). This is exemplified through the projects launched by Alfonso Femia at the time he began 'rethinking' his agency.

It was expressed by a mature architectural intention incorporating an awareness of the rapid changes taking place in urban development. Among these projects, it is worth mentioning the old Generali Properties building in Milan that the architect worked on to develop its coherence with the Porta Garibaldi station located at its base.

THE CORNER
▸ pp. 24-25, 46-47, 56-57, 110-111, 136-137, 156-157

The result anchors the Lombard metropolis into the hyper modernity of the 21st century. Initiated in 2004, this district has now become iconic thanks to its series of high-tech skyscrapers, the *Vertical Forest* high rise residential block and perhaps, most importantly, the reconciliation it embodies between Milan's historic centre and its contemporary districts. The renovated Generali Properties building has now found its place thanks to a new appearance, an added height and a more emphatic symbolic presence. For this project, Alfonso Femia sought to create a coherent identity for a patchwork of urban elements and give them new roles.

EUROPACITY, AFFORDABLE CHIC HOTEL 3*
▸ pp. 122-123

— Another concomitant project in 2017 saw Atelier(s) Femia, designing EuropaCity (winning project for an international competition) for the town of Gonesse. Apart from its functional intentions, the aim of this project was equally social and aesthetic. The programme was challenging: create a 450-bedroom hotel alongside a restaurant, co-working offices, various spaces for events, exhibitions and seminars, a spa and a fitness centre. Apart from being a building designer, the architect also needed to develop a strategy. His mission was almost impossible and consisted in assembling several cores and creating a 'village' from a group of buildings being used for different purposes that were not always well matched. The project called for cohesion and organicism as opposed to spatio-vital fragmentation.

Despite the challenge it represented, the EuropaCity project had the paradoxical advantage of forcing a confrontation with the contemporary world and, in particular, the management which had become highly fragmented over the occupant's life span. The multiplicity of services expected from this new project led to a 'chronotopical' approach. As opposed to the hermetic and isolated cluster approach, each building included in the new project was representative of a specific moment of our existences. The offices are occupied during the day, while the spa and fitness centre offer relaxation at the end of the working day. The restaurant is used at lunchtime and during the evenings, providing a warm and friendly atmosphere. By night, the hotel offers the perfect quiet moment during which social life can be shut down for a few hours.

"Within our design studios, we have a strong belief in the chronotopical city, a city able to interconnect the various moments of day to day life and create links with spaces. It is a contemporaneous approach that allows for different lifestyles" explains Alfonso Femia.
To 'chronotopically' design a set of buildings calls for them to be interdependent, linked to one another, easily accessible and that place considerable emphasis on fluidity. While this inevitably creates 'clusters', it also privileges continuity rather than discontinuous sequences. The aesthetics of this set of buildings with its various functions form part of the master plan (BIG and L35) and the wave-like urban continuity. It endeavours to be the figurehead of a three dimensional system that reveals waves which, despite their irregular rhythm, are all nevertheless linked to a single and same ocean. It is an allegorical representation of the primary ocean (where each individual lives among others), expressed as a vast and suggestive metaphor of the universal movement expressed as the addition of individual movements.

___ Atelier(s) Alfonso Femia's DNA? An architecture that is adapted, respects the order and seeks open dialogue with the client. It is a contextual architecture inseparable from its environment, an architecture that enhances close relations with a user that is always pampered. It is an architecture that takes an intense, radical and mental prospective approach that is always motivated by considerable generosity.

BNL-BNP PARIBAS HEADQUARTERS
▸ pp. 24-27, 34-35, 120-121, 142-143, 144-145, 152-153

— Rome provided yet another confrontation with the complication of reality. It is a difficult city in which to work, a setting that is both historical and contemporary, and an environment that is simultaneously structured and web-like. The project called for the construction of headquarters for the BNL-BNP Paribas bank in a district of the Eternal City sliced through by a railway line.
The majestic building designed by the architect (235 metres long, 12 superstructure floor levels and four basement levels, 42,000 square metres of usable floor area) purposefully adopted the appearance of a shell rising up alongside the railway lines. This bridge-building, the morphological equivalent of the phalanx of a giant finger, articulates two districts that had called out for reunification with, on the one side, the new Tiburtina station and, on the other, the Pietralata district.
Part of the façade of this monumental Janus is provided with a ceramic facing designed by Alfonso Femia and manufactured by Casalgrande Padana.
This use of noble materials and recognition of the skills of craftsmen and women is considered a principle expressed in all of Alfonso Femia's designs. In this particular case, the aim was to enrich the artistic *ratio* of an urban area that, while lively, lacked any particular qualities. Apart from its architectural prowess that has been rewarded by several prestigious prizes, the BNL-BNP Paribas head offices stand out for their sculptural intensity.
With their staggered layout and differentiated morphologies, the building's large number of glazed façades multiply the perspectives overlooking the city and its many urban marvels, much in the same way as a lighthouse reflecting the soul of Rome's skies.
With its presence, elegance, integration and homage, the new building creates the necessary 'link'. Apart from its practical efficiency, it brings together a number of dreams that, when assembled, result in an undeniable harmony.
Being an architect? Adding through architecture.

FROM ZERO TO INFINITY

— In terms of architecture and urban planning, Alfonso Femia's generation is familiar with theoretical debate. To have been trained in the 1980s and 1990s means having studied in an environment where a wide range of divergent options were expressed and required sorting. A reminder. At that time and still leading the field, the neo-modernists highlighted all the productivity of functionalism. Their Foster-based preference placed particular emphasis on infrastructures, as expressed through efficiency, profitability and austerity. The post-modernists, at that time beginning to topple modernist values, were more interested in historic citations, a return to traditions and had a clearly expressed taste for major references to an architectural past through pediments, porticos and other fluted columns dating back to antiquity: pleasant to look at, reassuring and easy, contagious. The deconstructivists, revealed by Philip C. Johnson at MoMA [1], pleaded their case for an architecture that, while not chaotic, should be as tormented as our rapidly changing planet. For these architects, crumpled, crushed and quirky buildings and towns torn apart were all able to express the uncertainties of today's world: impressive, eye-catching, stunning and astonishing, the concept increasingly convinced. It immediately joined the spectacular culture progressively being developed on a large number of screens and became engulfed in the digital entertainment culture. The biomorphists and subsequently the ecologists could only imagine the city of the future as one combined with data and other uncertainties forming part of

[1] "Deconstructivist Architecture", 1988, exhibition curated by Philip C. Johnson and Mark Wigley, at the MoMA of New York. Selected architects: Frank O. Gehry, Peter Elsenman, Zaha Hadld, Rem Koolhaas, Daniel Libeskind, Coop-Himmelb(l)au, Bernard Tschumi.

biological life and the natural environment. It was a city both futurist and vernacular, sophisticated and elementary, and increasingly in phase with a world suffering from global warming and environmental decay. And then, last but not least, there were those who were particularly keen on syntheses and who mixed everything together.

— A fair question for all young architect-urban planners confronted with this semantically disseminated plural offer: which way to turn? The juries of the prestigious Pritzker Prize themselves, rather than advocating a particular cause, sanctified them one after another.

One year it might be Jean Nouvel, an ardent and individualistic architect, while in another year, it could be Zaha Hadid, pioneer of a resurrected Soviet constructivism. Yet another year might see the sensible and reasonable Peter Zumthor advocating a return to a more modest existence or the lovingly programmed works of Alejandro Aravena, master of a culture of low prices and emergency architecture. The points of view differ greatly and the results are discordant. What to do?

— Put a lid on the boiling pot of theories, forget fashion and return to what is essential. Develop an architecture worthy of itself, worthy of its heritage, technology and symbolism. What might be imagined for today's and tomorrow's architecture?

— In general cultural history, the architecture of the early 21st century reveals an unequalled richness. Inventive, occasionally capable of breaking away from the traditions of the past to adopt other, more modern ideas, it provides a sign revealing the excellent state of health of a profession open to a wide range of possible futures.

Alfonso Femia approaches this wide range of possibilities by establishing priorities. Among the most important of these was to put a lid on the boiling pot of theories, forget fashion and, if not start over, then at least return to the essentials.
In so doing, what would be the expression of an architecture *worthy of itself*, worthy of its history and heritage, its technology and symbolism?
A first response lies in a demand for quality, a quality that Italian builders have proven able to provide since ancient times. The second response lies in adapting the architectural project to the programme.
The third lies in respecting the order, the budget, completion times and the certifications introduced in the 2000s that needed to be adapted to architecture – rather than the other way round.
The fourth was to take public expectations into consideration.
The fifth and final response was to provide an aesthetic that matched the local psyche, an approach aiming to give the architectural project a social as well as a transitional dimension.
While cultivating realism is a good thing, it is also worthwhile cultivating an open-ended imagination.

__ This multi-entry approach developed under the umbrella of 'imaginary realism' was adopted by Alfonso Femia very early in his career as an architect and urban planner and, given its success over the years, he simply updates it for every new project. Begun in the early 2010s (the first architectural project won in France), the rehabilitation of the Marseille Docks bears witness, should it be necessary, of the permanence of the agency's founding choices. Rehabilitating the Marseille Docks, a linear warehouse stretching out over 365 metres and located on the intersection of the historic city and the ancient Joliette port district, was not an easy exercise. In particular, it called for making the rehabilitated site, currently undergoing reconstruction, into Marseille's new epicentre. The Docks resemble a gigantic hangar – a wall facing onto the Mediterranean. The question asked was why not take advantage of a heritage so rich in potential in terms of content and

THE MARSEILLE DOCKS
▸ pp. 22-23, 28-29

physical presence. In answer to a programme demanding that standards be upgraded and a mix of hospitality supports and dozens of commercial units be incorporated, Alfonso Femia's response as a responsible professional was to respect the order. He nevertheless enlarged the initial balance of amenities. Within the heart of the building, he added four courtyards, each of which given a different identity. The intention was to vary the atmospheres and offer a rhythm and a specific image to an architecture that had initially been uniform and designed without care for aesthetics or narrative opening. Previously the front line between the old and the new Marseille, the rehabilitated Docks building can now be crossed through in different places and at different heights within the interior squares using public walkways. The warehouses are no longer a barrier. One of the side flanks giving onto a public square has now been provided with a pale coloured wall acting as a sunbreaker. Much in the same way as *moucharabieh* and Spanish mantillas, it is provided with an openwork finish in the form of the letters forming the Roman alphabet. The thousands of small openings in the wall become a stencil whose size matches that of the building and resembles the pages of a book. Passers-by progressively come upon a mass of phrases borrowed from literary texts making reference to Marseille. The result is a powerful relationship to the local context and the imagery it engenders. The building 'recites' the city. Here it is incorporated into a flourishing mythological tradition reflected by the particularly verbose Mediterranean soul. The rehabilitation of the Docks in Marseille by Atelier(s) Femia, which has already been awarded a number of prizes [2] , forms part of a physical and mental offer acting as a link between the past and the present of Marseille. The transformation of the Docks building, a constructed perimeter familiar to all those living in the city, in no way blocks its geographical setting which has now been enlarged to incorporate the entire district while simultaneously giving it a certain gloss and polish. As well as creating a link with the past, this transformation adds a reinforced identity aspect that takes the form of an additional sensitivity that goes far beyond any statuary change.

[2] MIPIM Awards for 'best shopping center'; first prize in the 'renovation' category of The Plan International Awards; ULI Global Awards for Excellence

__ There is no such thing as a ready-made architecture that, like Athena, emerges ready-armed from the thigh of Zeus. There are circumstances, needs and means to be evaluated and incorporated, and above all, intermediaries such as the user and the landscape. There are compromises to be negotiated. The architect must accept being the conductor, the person able to bring together occasionally cacophonic partitions within the same piece of music.

A CULTURE OF GIVING

— Architecture is a kind of gift. It is gift that can be both public and civic when, commissioned by the highest public authority, it offers citizens a building open to the public, be it a temple from an ancient past or a modern multimedia library. It becomes a private and intimate gift when this same architecture seeks to satisfy the desires of private individuals through the construction of residences or palaces. Architecture gives, but what exactly does it give? And who in fact "gives" in the process of its development: the client or the architect – or both at the same time?

— Let us not forget that a building, no matter what its purpose, has an end-user. Who or what is the architect's final perfect client? In fact, everything depends on the context or, to be more precise, what is being sought as the context.

[1] Robert de Luzarches (v. 1160 – 1228), medieval architect

[2] Michael VIII Palaiologos (v. 1224 – 1282), Byzantine emperor

When Robert de Luzarches [1] designed his masterpiece, the Notre-Dame cathedral in Amiens, he clearly had in mind that, above all, his client was God himself. His cathedral was intended to be the earthly response to the New Jerusalem spoken of in John the Apostle's Apocalypse. In parallel, Michael VIII Palaiologos [2], the all-powerful Caesaropapist sovereign of Byzantium, determined the architecture and decor of Middle Eastern Christian churches. Once again, the intention was to please the Christian god and provide what the Bible commanded in terms of the plan, organization and decoration of sanctuaries. However, the situation that might be called secular is more complex when the architecture serves a public authority, a utilitarian function or service, or even an individual whim. The Palazzo Te, a masterpiece designed by Giulio Romano [3] and pride of the aristocratic Frederick II family led by the marquis and then the Duke of Mantua, or the Taj Mahal, a sumptuous tomb born of the Moghul Shan Jahan emperor's desire to leave a monument for his deceased wife, are both examples of a personal passion, buildings that were for the exclusive use of their owners. On the other hand, New Harmony designed by Robert Owen [4] and the Guise cooperative designed by Jean-Baptiste André Godin [5] owe their existence and configurations to the principle of a shared living space and the pooling of the fruits of work. The destination of these two socialist inspired works, despite their eminent social goal, was not to concern society as a whole, given that they were both community-based. What can be learned from these various examples? No matter what the architecture, context is always a decisive factor. This context is less homogenous than heterogeneous as from the moment when one or the other powers, be they public or private entities, begin to multiply or even reveal that they are dissatisfied or become competitors.

[3] Giulio Romano, (v. 1492 or 1499 – 1546), Italian architect and painter

[4] Robert Owen (1771 – 1858), entrepreneur and British socialist theorist

[5] Jean-Baptiste André Godin (1817 – 1888), French industrialist

___ Architecture gives – with generosity as well as with reason. It is based on a principle of action-reaction. The gift of the best results in a counter-gift of satisfaction. In their own particular way, architects are patrons.

__ Atelier(s) Alfonso Femia always aims to achieve the objective of making the architectural offer into an act of 'giving'. An architect taking on a project should propose a building that simultaneously matches the demand and is generous. The principle of generosity, being the higher form of giving, permeates each of Alfonso Femia's projects. Discernable from the most humble to the most majestic of the missions awarded to the architect, generosity is the very DNA of the project.

Under these circumstances, offering relies on an ethic based on a desire to improve and enrich any given situation.

SAN GIOVANNI EXHIBITION CENTRE
▸ pp. 44-45

The San Giovanni exhibition space built in Casarza Ligure is a small arts centre constructed from cubic forms and provided with generous openings. The space offers an unparalleled charisma and stands out in what is otherwise a dull urban context. The toy museum in Cormano is naturally intended to appeal to children and is designed to remain closely tied to the world of childhood. Its raised entrance symbolically places it at a considerable distance from the real world. Accessed by a staircase reminiscent of Jack's magic beanstalk, the museum places emphasis on connections with children, providing play spaces for them to enjoy. The architecture here is a particularly dense entity and acts as a vector for an even greater sensitivity. In addition, Alfonso Femia imposes a further condition on his architecture: never design the same building in two different locations (no context being the same from one site to another). The buildings and urban planning projects designed until now by the architect refuse any form of repetition. This option also has the effect of reinforcing the generosity principle.

TOY AND ARTS FACTORY
▸ pp. 42-43

As a guarantee of diversity and attractiveness, each design, derived from a blank page, a context and the always specific nature of the demand, merge together through a dual conceptual basis. On the one hand, there is the adaptation which is the decisive factor in ensuring the relevance of the project; on the other hand, a generous practical and sculptural offer makes the project into something that is friendly rather than just useful.

DALLARA ACADEMY
▸ pp. 14-15, 20-21, 36-37, 112-113

— In autumn 2018, Atelier(s) Alfonso Femia handed over the Dallara Academy in Varano de' Melegari, a town not far from Parma where engineering students visit for excellence training courses in the field of mechanical arts. Could this be defined as a 'friendly' proposal? Without any doubt.

The Dallara Academy is a medium-sized circular building (5,000 square metres located near the entrance to 'Motor Valley' (near the Lamborghini and Ferrari plants), right next to the Dallara establishments, a company that has been designing racing cars since 1972 (particularly Formula 3 and Formula IndyCars in the United States). Commissioned by Gian Paolo Dallara, the historic founder of the company bearing his name, this new space is dedicated to education and, in particular, the training of racing car specialists. The AF517 offer for Dallara, with its emphasis on 'plus' and 'friendliness', called for a complete redesign of the initial project following discussions with the client. Although designed for educational purposes, the question was raised as to why not take advantage of the new structure and go beyond the activities of the internationally known Dallara name and use this made-to-measure building to expand the firm's activities. For a very reasonable cost, Alfonso Femia designed a signature building in the form of a cylinder pierced in its centre by two cones with truncated tops reaching towards the sky. This particular geometry was chosen because it followed a 'three in one' principle. The expansion of the architectural proposal had the effect of increasing the site's functionality. While the Dallara Academy remains an educational centre with the incorporation of several study spaces laid out inside the new building, it is also a museographical site that will serve to attractively display Gian Paolo Dallara's collection of cars which includes the legendary Lamborghini Miura (voted as the best car designed in the 20th century, it was designed by the Dottore of Varano de' Melegari who in 1966 was a young mechanical engineer). To that end and lying behind a glazed arrowslit façade, a circular rising ramp is used as an exhibition and discovery space that evokes the curve of a car circuit. This dynamic layout gives the building a sense of 'speed'. Finally, another function of the new building, as developed by the Femia 'method', is its connection to the local landscape. Research into colours was carried out, with the various colours of the new building echoing those of the surrounding flowerbeds.

In addition, the very proportions of the new Dallara Academy make it the focal point of a visual route incorporating the 'Motor Valley' located towards the bottom of the site and overhung by a majestic rocky outcrop.

— Awarded top prizes before it was even opened (ABB LEAF Awards 2017), the Dallara Academy stands out for its humility, inventiveness (several wall finish techniques have been tested on site), its precious nature and, even more so for the user, the immediate familiarity generated by its fluid layout that, at a single glance allows all the contents of the building to be immediately perceived. It offers a subliminal reminder of the 'continuous space' theory that appealed so much to the futurists who were fascinated by racing cars and everything that defied immobility. In this building built to a human scale, those entering immediately feel at home and are exposed to a pleasant feeling of completeness. The virtues of a 'friendly' building.

"Something stops you and something else reaches out. This, with its own dichotomy, is how the project develops. Concentrating on a subject provides an opportunity to dialogue with the various identities that form all architectural projects. I find that this sort of contamination creates dialogue".

Alfonso Femia

A SENTIMENTAL ARCHITECTURE

— The concept of 'caring' in the *corpus* of architectural cornerstones is considered to be ancillary, unlike those of service, adaptation and integration, or those more concrete concepts of form and proportion, which currently play a major role. This anomaly needs to be remedied. It is clear that designing architecture as being caring ('friends' of the site and of the user) is not the architect-urban planner's immediate concern. What should be the priority? Firstly, to provide protection and public spaces in which to shelter, move around, work and exchange as efficiency as possible. Is it really that inappropriate to make an architectural or urban planning project friendly? The concept of 'well-being', being the extended form of comfort, is always the result of a user-friendly transport system, alongside a feeling of belonging and friendship. In their own way, buildings are also 'individuals' and interlocutors. As an architect, how to offer friendship when handing over a building? The first obligation is to have a primordial respect of the users. The second obligation is to question the meaning of the project: what does the client really want, expect and dream of having? The third and probably the most important obligation is to ensure that the project opens onto 'happiness'.
— For Alfonso Femia, contributing to the happiness of 'occupying' is a categorical imperative. Here, the architect's peninsular culture plays a major role given the considerable mental references exposed to the full light of day and where the link between well-made objects and a feeling of achievement is patent. Italy is an excellent example of a *cose belle* country, a country

of beautiful things. This is held to mean ordinary things that have been made beautiful, that have been given a superior nature. They can range from the moka pot designed by Alessi just there to be admired without being used, through to the raised exhaust pipes of the MV Agusta F1000 that take the form of four sleeves resembling reactor shafts that inevitably attract and impress people. Transcendence is to be found throughout, including in the most commonplace objects. However, this familiarity with creative beauty has transitional consequences. It encourages the sharing of that which is attractive and has a highly positive effect on our awakened senses. It provides an invitation to create a common asset that can be integrated into a general culture. It is a way of making the world friendlier through the socialisation of beauty and, it goes without saying, enhancing beauty inevitably leads to a wider circle of admirers.
A compelling example of a 'friendly' architecture among others designed by Alfonso Femia is the restructuring of the Milanese Ice Factory, a real estate operation built in the Lombard capital in the early 2000s. Formerly a suburban ice-making factory lying alongside a skating rink, it had everything needed to be defined as an architectural headache. How to rehabilitate, how to reallocate this imposing concrete and scrap metal wreck that apparently is in a state of irreversible coma? What is more, how to change it into a 'friendly' structure that people will want to visit and share with others? The project developed by Alfonso Femia begins by joining together the building and the street, with the latter being used for the creation of 'social' outbuildings (including a café).

MILANESE
ICE FACTORY
▸ pp. 114-115

This operation is intended to 'civilise' the project and create a new urban hub. The historic skating rink lying below a glazed roof is conserved. In its renovated state and outside the winter season, it becomes an exceptionally well-lit exhibition space.
A tactical refurbishing project will take place in the interiors of the main building as well as on the untouched exteriors which will be repainted in a way that reduces the visual mass.
Reorganised and made lighter, their new presentation will also provide a considerable increase in the light entering the building.

A 'side opening' giving access to the upper floor levels has been created, the surface areas expanded, and balconies fixed to the building's east façade.
The emphasis placed on dual aspect lighting has resulted in greater attractiveness for the users who find themselves provided with a new, practical and flattering environment.

__ As an architect, it is necessary to accept being small if smallness is the condition to be met to achieve harmony. We need to facilitate, assume society's metamorphosis, and create a contemporary approach to the creation of links with the territory by banishing all forms of aggressiveness. Being fragile does not mean being weak. We are not eternal and fragility is part of the human essence. It is necessary to be builders rather than destroyers of 'worlds'.

[1] Alain de Botton, "The Architecture of Happiness", Pantheon Books, New York, 2006

__ In a study that marked a milestone, Alain de Botton [1] suggested the merits of the marriage between architecture and happiness. This potential alliance that we experience each time that a building gives us a feeling of wellbeing is never guaranteed. Castel del Monte, designed to embrace our bodies, enchants us, there where the Palace of Versailles looks down, resulting in the crushing and killing all simple happiness. In their own particular period, the situationalists would have said 'psychogeography' or complex of the real. Happiness, in our relationship to architecture, is far from automatic. While we are delighted to wander through the narrow passageways of the Ideal Palace designed by Facteur Cheval in Hauterives, the view over Corviale, the second longest modern housing block in Europe, is quite dreadful. Architecture, like the landscape, solitude, encounters and sex, concentrates on its side of happiness and its side of fear. Putting all considerations of personal taste to one side, who could deny that we are discouraged by Brasilia and enchanted by the town of Lucca? On the one hand, we have an excessive and inhuman urban layout hidden away in the Amazonian forest while, on the other hand, a priceless network of lanes and intertwining houses in the heart of Tuscany. The effects on our susceptibilities differ considerably. In the former case, they are locked down while, in the latter, they thrive.

__ Concerning architecture's capacity to produce happiness, a cardinal datum is required in connection with the spatial and the mental, being the sympathetic proximity between ourselves and the built space. A happy architecture is one that is close to us, that reflects our expectations and reveals itself favourable to the creation of wellbeing, serenity and the lightness of being. It belongs to us and, in turn, we belong to it. It is an exchange of feelings, passion, sensuality, beauty, spirit and real life.

__ In this instance, proximity is equal to cerebral comfort, physical ease and reciprocity: it is a tailor-made, made for me architecture, not in an abstract, normative and finally unsuitable manner (Le Corbusier's *Modulor*) but rather one able to enfold the individual. When in the 1940s, Hitler commissioned Albert Speer to design 'Germania', the new Berlin, he asked him to incorporate avenues that were wider than those constructed by in Moscow by Stalin, Hitler's sworn enemy. He also demanded that the dome over the future People's Hall, a pompous copy of Agrippa's Pantheon, should reach higher than the Eiffel Tower. The proximity between architecture and the users of the architecture in the monstrous case of 'Germania' was in no way included in the programme. Totalitarian power is always configured in such a way that it distances citizens who have vowed obedience.

They become ordinary subjects who need to assume their presumed place as slaves and servants. This is quite the opposite of the voluntarily small garden cities in England and Holland initiated in the 20th century. These cities, indifferent to any megalomaniac delusion, were more familiar and less oppressive when it came to the sensations linked to their use. Their scale respectfully reduces to our own scale while avoiding any humiliation. The new library in La Spezia, designed by Alfonso Femia, exudes happiness and, like the garden cities, leaves no place for excess, ostentation or architectural tyranny. It is a small, restrained linear building based on utility, simplicity and the avoidance of decorative finishes.

CIVIC LIBRARY
▸ pp. 30-31

Within these premises, nothing takes the place of reading or documentary consultation which remain the library's most important and privileged activities. Coarsely expressed, the building does not take priority over the way it is used.

The same observation can be made concerning the former great railways workshops in Turin that the architect reconfigured to celebrate the 150 years since Italy's unification (2011).

GREAT RAILWAYS
WORKSHOPS
▸ pp. 52-53

Most of the main building has been retained given that the aim of the general layout was intended to highlight the historic heritage of modern Italy. The main courtyard, partially paved with areas of red, evokes national passion and its flag, but without excess. The various rooms receiving visitors have been laid out in a way intended to provide reassurance and favour pacification rather than tension. The building expresses a language of reason and maturity and successfully keeps all orms of aggression at a distance: it is my friend.

__ Happy architecture is on the rise. A responsible and generous involvement in the project, on condition that it seeks friendship, places happiness within easy reach. Everything must be tried to this end, at the risk of making errors. The willingness is there.

RICH SUBSTANCE, PRECIOUS MATERIALS, PROXIMITY

__ All projects built by Alfonso Femia count on the interhuman link, no matter what the scale at which the architect operates. This can be seen within the framework of master plan types of projects. The Bry-Villiers-Champigny-sur-Marne urban planning scheme (Grand Paris Express programme) provides a good example. As imagined by Alfonso Femia, it includes the creation of an urban boulevard able to provide links between the various poles to be found in this conurbation located within the Paris region that, until now, had been spatially segmented.

PROGRAMMING AND URBAN STUDY
▸ pp. 48-49

The goal, as opposed to the territory's dense grid, is to offer a breathing space. It means the end of spatial isolation and the introduction of porous traffic movements and the intensification awaited from these exchanges. For users, it means a new relationship to an urban space that has become less distant, less strange and more personal. While proximity is a geographical fact, it is also a sensation.

Regarding the search for proximity, it is worth mentioning the set of buildings to be found in Asnières-sur-Seine (ZAC des Bords-de-Seine) bearing the evocative name of Gardens of Gabriel and which includes three housing blocks and a shop. While the scale is more reduced than in the preceding case, a same approach is taken of offering a differentiated setting that 'speaks' the idiom of an advantageous situation to its users. The construction of the new Gardens of Gabriel designed by Alfonso Femia counteracts a height that is too great, a certain coldness and popularisation. In its place, a renewed relationship with the environment is proposed: "The project was developed

THE GARDENS OF GABRIEL
▸ pp. 38-39, 140-141

"I incorporate ceramics, angels and butterflies in my buildings. I cut and trim to create links between public and private spaces. Understood in this manner, architecture becomes a form of education – a sentimental education. It creates dialogue.
Aesthetics are insufficient".

Alfonso Femia

by being based on an analysis of potentialities: atmosphere, the light of the landscape, environmental constraints and a formal game consisting in a series of cuts, openings and shifts defining the building's three main parts. The town is in constant dialogue with the interior park, resulting in the creation of a rhythm between the built elements and the landscape. The project's architectural style is based on a concept of rhythm (openings, materials and handling of the upper floors). Within a shared grammar, it favours the diversity of an urban landscape created between the town and the natural environment". In addition, six sculptures of angels distributed throughout the building and in the garden welcome residents or those visiting. The angels also act as an opening to the imagination underlying the name of the setting that makes reference to Gabriel, the most important of the Gospel's messengers. It is an effect of the 'imaginary realism' lavishly used in the Atelier(s) Femia's architectural designs. It is worth clearly mentioning here, and particularly because it is linked to the search for proximity, the work carried out by Alfonso Femia on and with materials, being a subject that particularly fascinates him (right through to the theoretical level, as can be read in the pamphlet entitled *5+1AA Architectures Rights and Duties*, 2014). [1] This can particularly be seen in the programme for the Gardens of Gabriel: "particular attention is paid to the choice of materials. The project is characterized by the reaffirmation of the decor through the use of ceramics and the ornamentation of the façades". The architect's objective is to distance uniformity while simultaneously opening the building onto the 'sky", with the latter being the term used within the agency to designate the aim of the project. The appearance of the ceramic finishes over the building's façade changes with the colours and light adapting to the seasons and the time of day. In this area, it acquires a structural role that goes beyond the decorative principle. "The various brick layouts and the employing of different geometries using a same material enrich the façade without weighing it down", notes the architect. "The joinery picks up and reinforces the colours of the façades,

[1] Paul Ardenne, Alfonso Femia, Gianluca Peluffo, "5+1AA Architectures, Rights and duties", Venezia, Marsilio Editori, 2014

using brick slips and rendered frames. The articulation of the materials enriches the composition of the façades".
In this specific case, working with materials having this particular strength of calculated correlations and contrasts can be seen as work within the work. This work carried out on details, not necessarily seen at first glance, has the discreet but decisive function of 'refining' the building, giving it a subtlety that lightens both its mass and function.
In his relations to materials, Alfonso Femia lays claim to be both Italian and French but also – and particularly – to belong to *mare nostrum*. He has cultivated a taste for delicate ornamentation as might be enjoyed in Italy or Paris and avoids the excesses of the Baroque, the cult of knick knacks and the frigidity of modernism. Multiplying the number of different materials, working on them and giving them a strong identity is not a masking fig leaf successfully or unsuccessfully disguising the poverty of an architecture but rather a way of offering the project a positive dimension that must tell a story. Then, the formula of Edvard Munch can be used, "Tale is the objective of every art creation".

__ It is necessary to counter Adolf Loos. Ornamentation is not a crime if it avoids ostentation and makes details into structural components of the architecture. Decor is never free of charge. It is important that it be embodied in materials chosen for their capacity to amplify the architectural offer while avoiding any kitsch or sensationalism. Action and exultation.

THE VAULTS
OF ALGIERS
▸ pp. 126-127

__ The reconfiguration of the vaults in Algiers (2017) in the heart of the Algerian capital has the same concern of bringing people closer to the location. This time, the sought objective was to increase the intimacy of the space by creating an intermediate scale lying between residential housing and urban project. This esplanade, created in the 19th century by the French coloniser, over-densely built and crowded, had become unreadable as a result of ad hoc redevelopment projects. Alfonso Femia and his Atelier(s) took a radical approach to the project by opting to tear down the fabric.
Two buildings interrupting the access and views over the sea were demolished. A complete redevelopment was undertaken to recreate the sea front and its promenades that had been widened to provide space for pedestrian areas.
This project and many others generally described in these pages merit being looked at in greater detail. Simply for this reason, there is a constant concern for 'details' to be found, being the 'details' so dear to Paul Valéry's Eupalinos [2]. This mythic architect believed, with reason, that a large-scale project is, as well as being a whole, a sum of parts.
Concerning the particular importance placed on details by Atelier(s) Femia, it is worth mentioning the amount of work put into light and lighting. This work is often carried out in consultation with, among others, the Castaldi Lighting company, for which Alfonso Femia, as an inventive designer, creates layouts and projects. Or, equally, there is the fruit of detailed research into materials used in a large number of buildings signed by AF517 alongside the integration of rare materials, ceramics, brushed and anodised metals and other complex finishes whose virtue is to capture light and adapt the ambient atmosphere in function of the sun's movement across the sky or resulting from urban night-time lighting, such as can be seen, for example with the Gardens of Gabriel operation. 'Resubstantialise' or, to define it in another way, 'to put back substance'. Why this persistence? To counter the absence of the substance that is characteristic of 'junk spaces' to be found

[2] Paul Valéry, "Eupalinos ou l'Architecte", 1921

in contemporary cities that are saturated with advertising, obstacles and grime. As defined in the dictionary, 'substance' is 1, 'that which is permanent' (as opposed to that which changes), 2, 'that which is essential (in a thought, a written composition, etc.)'. Thus defined, 'substance' engages both the issue of immutability and essentiality. Substance continues to exist over time and is resistant to wear, decay and entropy. Because its substance is unquestionable, it cannot be ordinary. Substantiating architecture is to densify it, increase its proximity potential using a dialogical mode between what is built and the physical presence of the user. Once 'substantialised', the building emits the equivalent of a 'living entity' and interacts considerably with our perceptions and feelings.

__ The choice of a material cannot depend on fashion. The material is an active agent that makes it possible to avoid indifference, levelling and repetition. It singularises architecture by making it an art of sensitive arrangements. Refinement is welcome.

WORKING FOR OUR BODIES

— The classic cornerstones of architecture are to be found in the human body. In *De Architectura* (First century BC), Vitruvius, a master mason, maintained that the initial search for harmony between humans and the shelter they seek for protection is firstly a matter of measurement and, more specifically, the measurement of the body itself. According to this great Roman architect, the body is the basis for the building, which should be the envelope, the extension and the shell; in other words an exoderm that is simultaneously able to be useful, practical and obliging. For the substance from which the body is made, the 'appropriate' architecture (in other words 'adapted'), rather than offering a risky envelope should present itself as a complementary substance linked to the equally organic human substance. The building is nothing less than the armed and protective extension of our flesh and bones, and our lives. Concerning the fundamentals of Atelier(s) Femia, to emphasise the importance of the 'substance' concept is to bear witness to the inexorably humanist choices made by the agency. A good example of this taste for a humanist architecture, in a somewhat biased but significant manner, is provided by the attention that Alfonso Femia pays to the 'music' of buildings. Designing a building could mean finding its best 'musical' modulation, a musicality able to contribute to encouraging an agreeable relation to the built environment. Let us consider the building as a piece of music. As such, it can be insipid and repetitive (tall blocks), light (a small sunlit cottage overlooking the sea), transcendental (the Hassan II mosque in Casablanca), etc. Alfonso Femia also proposes that the building should be appreciated as "a constant musical pentagram, a setting where rhythm and sequence, whether vertical or horizontal, permit the story he has created to be narrated". It is therefore up to the architect to use the geometry of this acoustic pentagram to be found in every building. For AF517, it is not to the profit of any particular music: first and foremost, even exclusively, it is one that privileges musical clarity and therefore a conceptual and narrative clarity. This 'musicalist' approach is not purely formal. It is more than the basis for a dinner table argument or rhetorical discussion. This was the approach that guided the architect when, within the physical framework of the École Centrale of Marseille, he was asked to incorporate a Creativity Center (2018). This was a 'musical' project that resulted from a rehabilitation developed with, once again and as a central focus, the well-being of the users who, rather than being served with a symphony, a requiem or an aria, were offered something far more discreet and considerably more immersive. The point of departure was a modernist concrete building as long as a month of Sundays and forming a wing as uniform as a note held by Philip Glass. It was a building that had to represent a cantata or at least an attractive music. The option chosen by Alfonso Femia was one based on chamber music. "Bringing life back to an abandoned setting and giving it a fresh look without shedding the envelope were the maxims guiding this rehabilitation project that called for creativity rather than construction. The architectureis a vector for poetry, enthusiasm and emotion. It cannot leave people feeling indifferent. Its purpose is to provoke the senses and sharpen sensations". Chamber music? The external face of the building, revitalised by the coloured treatment of the façades and flanked by a staircase that makes the space more welcoming, acts as a prelude to the interior layout which is particularly open and clearly organised while also providing access to a number of separated spaces used for reflection, studies, private communications and small groups. Multitudes of sonatas are played here and there in the heart of the building in accordance with the occupation of the spaces. If there is a symphonic temptation, then it finds itself expressed in the main auditorium but in a spirit of seriousness that excludes *Les Troyens* by Berlioz (too thunderous), while placing emphasis on the cerebral (the

MC2
CREATIVITY CENTER
▸ p. 58

final quartets by Beethoven): dominant clarity, calculated restraint. In its own way and through its own particular style, architecture is an art of sounds. Music again? The conversion of the former infantry training school in Montpellier (6,150 square metres, 82 rehabilitated housing units) once again gave Atelier(s) Femia an opportunity to express its taste for scores, a term that once more should be understood in a musical sense. The former infantry training school, in its diagrammatic layout, is a restrained 19th century, five floor construction that is neither massive nor lightweight. Built in the 19th century French administrative style, it is a building that is restrained, serious, classical, formally laid out, given rhythm, provided with high ceilings and designed to last. The 'music' produced by this building is fairly monotonous, a little military and somewhat loud. How to allow this building to sing better? Accompanied by the nearby construction of new buildings, the decision was taken that the rehabilitation should rise up an octave: just a little higher, just a little clearer. The interior layout has been redesigned with, in particular, the introduction of a monumental staircase signifying the building's change of use and the return of a more luminous life, one that is soprano rather than mezzo. The roof is the setting for overhanging housing units with enlarged ridges embedded into the existing roof much like large dormers. The whole takes the form of a joyous coping. It now executes a cantata while the design of the façade, particularly marked by horizontal lines, is left with its initial tonality, being the equivalent of a basso continuo, and offering a more austere and ceremonial tone. While the original spirit of the setting is respected, its attraction is increased and magnified. With an amplification mode that refuses any hubbub, the building 'rings' better.

EAI SITE
▸ pp. 50-51

__ A building is a physical object that can wisely be made into a relational object. All constructions engender their own signatures and musicality. Designing an architecture imposes considered research into sensitive relationships and, to this end, the harmonisation of relationships with the territory, the town, the users and the local mythology.

— While it is not certain that there exists an architecture of happiness that can remain happy over time, there is however an architecture of unhappiness. What criteria can be used to define this architecture? It could be the violence exercised against the environment, providing proof of user discouragement.
The cause of a negative sensation with regards architecture lies in the unsubstantialised or badly substantialised nature of the building and in the little consideration expressed by this architecture for our physical presence. Refusing an architecture that is a-substantial, without substance or having a substance right on the edge of what is inorganic, is now, in an antinomic and declared manner, equivalent to the promotion of care which is nothing less that the 'ethic of concern' that has become one of our brutal era's major concerns. As opposed to a culture of disdain or violence, the role of architecture is to do good and offer a greater well-being. The application of this positive virtue was expressed in the mission given to Alfonso Femia and his Atelier(s) for the remodelling of the MSC Cruises head offices in the building known as the 'Three Towers' located in a not particularly pleasant part of Genoa's commercial port. Alfonso Femia gave this old building positioned in the San Benigno district a reflective veneer prior to cladding the large exterior staircases and balconies, being an aesthetic drive that did not contradict the general aesthetics (the building's ecological impact is more than guaranteed). As explained by the architect: "The underlying idea for the new project was to use stained glass to obtain a colour gradient over all the façades of the three towers, resulting in pale tones on the sides least exposed to the sun and darker colours on the most exposed facades. These characteristics help to meet the regulatory obligations imposed by law concerning energy savings". In addition, concerning

THREE TOWERS
IN SAN BENIGNO
▸ pp. 18-19, 132-133

the ecological and delicate aspects of this operation taking place in Genoa: "In all, six colours are used; two by two, tone on tone, with the idea that each of the sides of the tower blocks be provided with a softer and less contrasted colour than that of the adjacent façade. The project uses two different colours of glass whose technical characteristics favour the respect of thermo-acoustic criteria imposed in this area and for this type of building". Previously the repulsive emblem of an era now long past (the present day port has been transferred to other shores), the redesigned building has been transformed and made welcoming. However, the building in no way denies its existence, anchorage or opening onto the sea. Here, the concept of care takes on its full meaning: restore rather than damage, support given to the living rather than weakening or humiliation. There is no destruction or alignment along the trivialised standard of the Central Business Districts. The new MSC Cruises head offices, through an 'imaginary realism', operates a winning metaphorical return to the world of Pittura Metafisica which is strongly involved in the local culture, providing a mix of proximity and distancing. Because of its stature, visibility and capacity to capture the vision, it remains a central element of the 'narrative' and the metaphysics of the Ligurian capital.

__ An urge to donate, a sense of friendship and happiness, substantialisation and a capacity to imagine. To fully define the 'method' used by Atelier(s) Femia, it is also necessary to include this other determining factor: a strong sense of opportunity. The building should merge with its location and its era. With the benefit of a century's hindsight, we know all too well how modern urban planning has mishandled the principles of friendship, donations, happiness and 'care'. 'Housing blocks', extravagant master plans that partition spaces by creating specialist uses (housing, work and leisure), car constraints and commuting, all those aspects inseparable from modernism, are now considered as ugly, creating an 'unfriendly relationship' with users who find themselves more exposed to discomfort than to pleasure. To once again make living and urban spaces into friendly environments, to counter an indifferent approach to the residents and replace it with a sense of well-being and developing a resistance to technocracy are now the missions expected to be carried out in opposition to all that has previously been done by architects and urban planners. There are four aspects to these missions: fluidify traffic, bringing people together, reducing congestion in living spaces, and interconnecting the various entrances that create social areas. These are the missions undertaken by Atelier(s) Alfonso Femia, missions carried out ostinato, 'millimetre by millimetre', as explains its founder. It is only on this condition and none other that the agency will continue its journey, carrying on the work begun by 5+1AA. It is an energetic and vigilant concept of 'journey' illustrated by the agency's logo, being a whale that, from its habitat in the depths of the ocean, looks up towards a star as it stretches its powerful body. Using its adaptive capacities, each project built by Atelier(s) constructs this journey. It goes without saying that the agency never turns away from the pitfalls of the contemporary world. On the contrary, it forces itself to assimilate their nature in order to better overcome them.

__ Encounters and exploration. Doubts vs certitudes. Questions vs answers. Opinions vs realities. Harsh realities vs imaginary realism. A question of integration into the future and responsibility. Organising knowledge and technical skills with the aim of sharing. Architecture transcends construction and, as Kant would have said, it is a "mathesis universalis", a philosophical act that involves thought as much as it does technology.

SOCIETAL SKILLS, MAKING THE IMAGINARY

__ During the summer of 2017, to carry out a rethinking exercise concerning an agency's (*Atelier(s) Alfonso Femia AF517*) continuum mode was an eloquent measure. We do not betray ourselves. We just continue – but we change gear. Refounding implies impetus, the tough continuity of the journey, the seeking of an energy that is resolutely turned towards a creative project that is more intense, more radical, sure of itself and its contents. The whale pursues its path between the ocean depths and the surface. It has escaped the Ned Land's [1] harpoon and is now ruler of its kingdom. The time has come for affirmation.

[1] Jules Verne, "Twenty Thousand Leagues Under the Seas", 1870

__ The architectural device at the beginning of the 21st century is undergoing considerable change. It needs to take social expectations as well as aesthetics into consideration. It also needs to see architects accepting that they are no longer 'emperors and masters of their kingdom'. Rather than being shameful, compromise is now a new organisational essence.

__ For Alfonso Femia, maturity is a question of choice. It is the refusal of a directionless weathervane approach that sees people carried away by every new fashion. Choice means giving priority to contextualisation, the specificity of each programme, dialogue and material, and to the inclusion of the imaginary, elegance and subtlety. The time has come for the sedimentation of concepts, and the incorporation of 'FF', the 'Femia Formula'.

The architect has changed from the Calabrian child that he was into an Italian who has since become a European.

THE GARDENS OF GABRIEL ▸ pp. 38-39, 140-141

THE MARSEILLE DOCKS ▸ pp. 22-23, 28-29

BNL-BNP PARIBAS HEADQUARTERS ▸ pp. 26-27, 34-35, 120-121, 142-143, 144-145, 152-153

This metamorphosis is not simply due to his moving from one place to another. Several competitions that were simultaneously won in the early 2010s – the housing in Asnières-sur-Seine, the Docks in Marseille, the BNP in Rome – allowed him to confirm the soundness of his approach (with preference given to the term 'approach' rather than that of 'style' which is overly influenced by the primacy of aesthetics). It is a sign that architectural imperatives, always suspected of missing in times of economic crisis and builder kings who confuse architecture and promotion, are back. These successes, absorbed by Atelier(s) Femia with both recognition and modesty, are also the sign that the agency's architectural direction and method match the dominant concerns of both private and public clients as well as those of users. An acknowledgement? At the very least. Among the salvo of new competitions won at the same time, certain of them already mentioned in these lines credit the 'Femia Formula' with a certain consistency. A tourist complex in La Ciotat next to Marseille, the former infantry school in Montpellier, the Pasteur site in the University of Avignon, the École Centrale of Marseille, EuropaCity in Gonesse in Paris's northern suburbs, the redevelopment and recovery of the complex of the first Italian State Mint in Rome, the offices on the Toulouse-Blagnac airport, the cruise terminal of La Spezia etc. Whether for rehabilitation works or the design of new buildings, the Atelier(s) offer rallies the choices of a large number of decision-makers.

Concerning this success story, rather than concentrate on an infatuation that would contribute to making him and his works

increasingly desirable, Alfonso Femia focuses on two Darwinist data that inevitably result in a natural selection. Firstly, explains the architect, the time is now upon us for a gradual return of aesthetics, a renaissance in the need for exactingness and clarity. For a large number of clients, this still means reducing costs and expectations within the local space-time environment with the attendant risk of a junk or pustular architecture laid like a carbuncle on a face.
However, rigour is essential if the intention is clearly to avoid further distorting the urban landscaping of our towns and villages. Those architects who do not subscribe to this demand for just a little more quality run the fatal risk of sooner or later simply vanishing, even if they agree to concessions.
For Alfonso Femia, another natural selection process, apart from waiting for the return of more ethics, is a refusal to organise the new promotion – design – construction scheme which has become less hierarchical than in the past. Whether they like it or not, 21st century architects will need to assume a deficit in functional representation. He cautions that "we will need to openly face what architecture will turn into and what it will be in the future. It is becoming a practice whose skills escape a growing number of architects.
Architects are no longer alone gazing at a blank sheet of paper. They now have to work with a promoter or developer among other players whose points of view cannot be dismissed out of hand. While architects remain central to a project, their position has ceased being sovereign. It is the end of architectural authoritarianism". How to better express the need within the organisation for greater flexibility and the acceptance of negotiations? Whoever refuses these new rules risks losing one competition after another. Architects no longer just have to wait for the red carpet to be rolled out as took place in the past for Bernini or, more recently, Ieoh Ming Pei, architects who just had to wait to be invited but never had to compete. "In the 2000s", continues Alfonso Femia, "I was able to see the effects of this metamorphosis, both in Italy and France. However, this

was accompanied by the risk of a process that could lead to architecture losing its value through decomposition.
As from now, the position of responsible architects is self imposed: respect the rights of the client and organisers while, without delay or weakness, negotiate architecture's right to play its role, without excessiveness or absolutism but rather with the authority needed by architects to assert their skills.
It is necessary to understand that this is a kind of battle. Initiating a battle for the project, in its favor and not against the contracting authority. In any way, it is about to impose a style or an architecture but to fight for the founding principles of the project and its viable arguments. To free the mind and develop ideas, it is essential that a project be given a specific direction and, to that end, must be strengthened and developed by being provided with solid supports. Achieving the battle means to never lose sight of the importance and the value of the project."
Alfonso Femia's success, this time based on philosophy rather than theory, can also be due to another reason that remains rational and which does not bear discussion in terms of legitimacy, being the civic sense.
His architecture seeks to be civic and involved in civil life.
To be brief, it plays the game of the call for responsibility that currently lies at the heart of general concerns, a demand that, specifically in the European Union of the 2000s, favours sociability. Rather than being isolated, rather than declaiming a solitary and onanistic score, architecture is improved by mixing with the world in all its diversity. To develop 'societal skills' is not a distortion. The continuity of collective life, as opposed to libertarianism and antisocial egoism, is the price to pay. But all this depends on a certain willingness.
At Atelier(s) Alfonso Femia, the principle takes the form of a commitment to society.
Either the architecture is inclusive or it is not worthwhile and should be left in the hands of solitary neurasthenics going round and round in circles.

__ There is an architectural ethic. It is collective and adheres to the concept of a joint contract and a life led in society. The challenge is to reject the harmful and antisocial evolution represented by the privatisation of the world. A moral building is a socialised material body.

__ Architecture as a factor of social cohesion. Consulted in 2015 within the scope of the construction of the Grand Paris project (at the time the largest construction site in Europe), Alfonso Femia clearly expressed his intention of ensuring that his moral and federating position prevailed. The study concerned the connection project for the new Créteil-L'Échat regional express railway (RER) station in Paris's eastern suburbs.
The new district, organised around this railway hub, designed to act as a beacon (there is a tower block over the station), needed to incorporate a number of amenities based on a mix of uses: offices, and hotels, as well as student and social housing over a 22,000 square metres surface.

CONNECTED PROJECT OF GRAND PARIS EXPRESS
▸ pp. 130-131

This small town within a town, built up around an infrastructure backbone, was designed by Alfonso Femia in discussion with Michel Guthmann, an associate architect. The choice was made to avoid a linear layout (urban amenities laid out along the tracks) and place emphasis on local urban development.
A non-metric network of streets, an accumulation of public and private spaces in the spirit of 'freespace', a refusal to accept any authoritarian prospects: the clearly expressed ambition is the search for a "balance between the urban role of the project (unit) and the identity of each of the component parts (sequence of uses)". "This clear-cut position is physically expressed by a line running parallel to the road that deviates and opens onto two courtyards. These give access, on the one hand, to the housing and, on the other hand, to the offices and residences (student

and hotel accommodation)", explains Alfonso Femia. "The project finds its form in an alternation of sequences that materialise on one or another of the built elevations, creating a system of urban scenes". In this setting with its vast number of openings, where the user transits almost at the speed of light, the social challenge is transformed.
It is the result of intensified circulation, permeability and the creation of occasional 'village effects'.

TOURISTIC COMPLEX
▸ pp. 146-147

— Designed in 2016, the cinema, leisure and sports centre in La Ciotat near Marseille provides a further example of architecture's contribution as a catalyst for socialisation and as an expression of the building's role in society.
The new complex, incorporating a cinema, a bar-restaurant, shops, a fitness centre and a hotel, places particular emphasis on the need to provide a mixed structure. Its aggregated nature systematically breaks down the spirit of segregation induced by the culture of the Athens Charter and enhances specific and distinguished living environments in function of human activity. Homogenous, structured like a networked whole, the building designed by AF517, with its restrained yet tenacious mass is given a certain lightness by its pale façades. One of them is fitted out with vertical vents, exposing the relevance of what are, a priori, heterogeneous groupings. What is more, located on the corner of two avenues, it operates as a landmark in the local urban fabric. It offers just the right level of monumentality without being arrogant and the right level of visibility without being overly humble. Lastly, it offers complete accessibility.
— Welcoming without being enclosing. Spaces need to be opened up rather than shut away. The restructuring of the Pasteur site in Avignon, including the construction of the Villa Supramuros ('the creative villa'), also forms part of this same approach. What is being sought by the clients? To perpetuate the 'reflection workshops' developed during the Avignon Festival and give them a clear-cut and separate framework. Once again, the challenge is to open out the space as much as possible to create settings where people can meet one another

and develop inter-human and inter-professional encounters. The point of departure is a typically early 20th century standard public building that is well built, without any particular qualities but which has a considerable heritage value in a rapidly changing urban environment. The site, resembling a 3rd Republic sub-prefecture, will be transformed into an activity hive bustling with state-of-the-art conferences, co-working spaces and the quiet hum of computers. One of the rehabilitation programme's constraints was to maintain the envelope while the inside of the building, containing several wings giving onto one another, could be redesigned with a far greater degree of freedom. For the Pasteur Site, Alfonso Femia chose an open 'lab' solution. The new laboratory space purposefully multiplies the number of units, breaks down spatial hierarchies and segments working spaces in the same way as an open space. Once again, circulation is the key word to the project. As well as providing a landmark for the town, notes the architect, "the Villa Supramuros also needs to develop bridges, links and interactions between both artistic and scientific disciplines to create a landmark for the town". Put another way, on a local level, its aim is to assume the role of being a total relational centre. "Fluidity, the development of a compact form of organisation, a time line approach, spatial prioritising, light management, etc. represent the interfaces, connections and areas of friction between the various centres that can result in an overall coherence. User-friendly spaces need to be given very careful thought to provide a warm environment that invites relaxation, sharing and exchanging. The garden plays an important role in this necessary creation of connections between users. As a real living space, its organisation contributes to the development of social interactions. To encourage ideas to grow and projects to germinate, users will find that these spaces offer centres of synergy allowing them to share their experiences". The restructuring of the Pasteur site in Avignon provides a lesson. Skilful work on the organisation of the various sections led to the creation of a new federating space:

"Rather than trying to create several programs within the same envelope, the aim was to have a single project structured around a shared idea, being that of interdependence between culture, digital sciences and research". It is worthwhile focusing on these words by the architect as the concepts of federation and interdependence are essential. Atelier(s) Femia's DNA intrinsically bases its programme on cohesive concepts that replace moral values. Here, the ethical line is represented by refusing separatism, isolationalism or 'retiring to an ivory tower'. In Common Contract societies where everyone is concerned by the law, architecture grows by contributing to the feeding of the common substance. There is a radical refusal to accept the development of large 'pompous and decontextualised' structures.

___ Architects are not demiurges. They do not battle against the world to impose their views. On the contrary and more generously, they organise their ideas in a way that harnesses disparate energies, allowing them to be included in their projects.

ACCOMPANYING CIVILISATION

__ There is also a refusal to use 'cut and paste' solutions to duplicate the same type of building or master plan. Turning his back away from seductive projects that are too closely married to fashion, he also refuses any simplistic or individualistic panderings. Architecture, according to Alfonso Femia is more easily defined by its experimental nature.
And as for repetition? *Not in my name.*
The previously discussed desire to avoid repetition is logical and results from motives linked to different contexts. Each context has its own particular resolution. Similarly, it also results from a clinical type of subjacent desire: to add nothing to the growing homogeneity of our planet, a world governed by globalisation, which by nature is anti-identity and erases local difficulties in exchange for indifference. Do we need *Dubai Kitsch* or *No Style For All*? No thanks. In a world that is globally globalised, everything tends towards the inorganic, from lifestyles through to ways of living and from taste to our mental structures. This standardisation can rightly be considered as a factor unfavourable for civilisation. In a fatal manner, it adapts all consciences to the most dominant powers while erasing specificities and 'differences'.
When universality becomes the bulldozer of identities, it would be better not to fuel the dehumanising evolution it instigates. The human being is a whole and, within this whole, is also the expression of a singularity that we must hope is irreducible.
__ This choice of not repeating, which does honour to AF517 – acronym for Atelier(s) Femia and, as can now be understood, is also the code name for their voyage and slow, daily battle – admittedly

has an unfortunate and inevitable consequence calling for a certain reflection: the difficulty in being identified; to be identified in a clear-cut manner, much in the same way as words that are repeated or a language impregnated. To be identified, at a moment in time when the architect and urban planner, like no matter what kind of producer in this world, should be the 'seller' as explained by architect and Pritzker Prize winner Rem Koolhaas. What is meant by that? Architects and urban planners must be singled out at any price, be made exceptional through their works or run the risk of not be visible and, consequently, unable to produce. Who in the construction process can deny the primary importance played by financing and insurance and the way they largely define the nature, size and aesthetics of buildings? It is also important not to forget the often invalidating public relations. Jean Nouvel in New York, for instance, had to lower his 53W53 skyscraper located near MoMA by 100 metres following an authoritarian decision made by the municipality and, notwithstanding a first agreement, it was determined that there was no question in this part of Manhattanto build higher than the venerable Chrysler Building. Thus, the need to 'sell oneself'. Without always going as far as venality or offering oneself the possibility of quick-fix solutions, asserting oneself often calls on architects and urban planners to develop their personal styles, specialisations or image. In a conference given at the Paris École Centrale in November 2012, Rem Koolhaas began his presentation by accompanying it with a view of the Parthenon. This building, he pointed out, was, for citizens living in Athens at the same time as Pericles, a 'collective asset'. He then asked: "what at present, in the early 21st century, is the building that we could equally call a 'collective asset'"? The Dutch architect then showed his audience an image of the Guggenheim Museum in Bilbao, Frank O. Gehry's masterpiece. He explained that although it is clearly a public building (a museum), it is empty (no permanent collection), simply a magnificent shell that is firstly an envelope and then a performance, a signature building. In other words, it is an extravaganza, the equivalent of a Hollywood blockbuster. AF517 or the refusal, we must acknowledge, of 'show-off' buildings. For this reason: if one is a friend of the planet, then it is necessary to look at it, infuse it and accept it for what it is. The architecture to be found across the world, and concerning the latter, needs to create symmetrically and avoid false reflections. For Alfonso Femia, this means no *trompe-l'œil* but rather an architecture that seeks to read between the lines of our era and its unflagging hope for a better sense of well-being, despite all setbacks and hurdles. While this might mean less glory, it matters very little if there is less deception. A building whose aim is to impress its users should be sanctified over time and by time. It should be lived in and experienced by people and create a flood of feelings. A building will have succeeded in impressing the day when history demonstrates that its soul has been developed in a free manner, always considering time to be one of the project's intrinsic components. __ We need to be aware of this, accept it, guide the building and await its development. The project needs time to express itself. Nor should architects be anxious insofar as their performance is concerned because, finally, the work is not intended for them.

__ Architecture needs to read what already exists, look towards the latter and then towards the imaginary. To this end, it needs to write the possible metamorphosis that shifts its gaze from the present to the future. It is important to maintain, reread and stage the building's founding elements. It is also important to give it a new soul at that moment in time when life once again occupies the setting and reappropriates the space.

— To be an architect and to be one in a virtuous manner calls for a creativity that respects the spirit of civilisation. There is something greater than us and that something overhanging us is the powerful matter called civilisation, a life developed not as an expression of non-control and brutality, but rather as a set of rules, attitudes and laws that allow us to live together harmoniously. In a discreet manner, the rehabilitation and enhancement of the covered market in Aosta (feasibility study, 2017) provides a striking example of a 'civilising' architecture that offers a net contribution to references of European civilisation, one of the most enlightened that currently exists. On a rectangular square flanked by residential buildings and with, on one side, the old covered market, Atelier(s) Alfonso Femia has designed a slender one-storey building that incorporates two retail spaces, one on the level of the square and the other on an upper level and overhanging the space below. The building has a lightweight wooden roof that is both gentle and curving, evoking the halls of medieval markets.

REDEVELOPMENT OF THE MARKET HALL ▸ pp. 150-151

This citation can be based on historicism by asserting that not everything forming part of traditions and heritage should necessarily be discarded. Above all, the building has the quality of pacifying the environment, with its form suggesting concepts of protection, hangar, abundance of the content and safety. The spatial layout also has an important role to play in this project. The new building is intended to be as closely connected to the town as possible, with its setting being organic and natural rather than artificially introduced. This option is completely contrary to the 'spectacularism' so characteristic of commercial architecture competitions. Early 21st century architects have notoriously revealed their particular enthusiasm for grandiose malls where the first criteria is to separate the building from its surroundings. "In our era, installing buildings of cultural interest is a question of responsibility", explains Alfonso Femia. The term is particularly important. Architecture is dialogical and raises the particularly central issue of belonging. Does this building belong to me, citizen of Genoa or Asnières-sur-Seine?

Any new architecture in a given setting rewrites the *genius loci* to ensure its fundamental essence. Firstly, in the name of this reason, there is the existence of a symbolic substrate to be taken into consideration and which imposes its views no matter whether or not appreciated. A Mediterranean, an Italian, a Parisian or a European cannot have the same vision, the same comprehension or the same expectations as an individual confronted with a spatial or human void.

Consequently, that which is created in a new universe, runs the risk of finding itself displaced in the effervescing cultural environment to be found in the Mediterranean-Europe region. The futility of memory in a new world as opposed to the saturation of memories accumulated in the ageing universe of the Old World (elderly by age, obviously, but surely not by its civilisation which is now leading in terms of human respect, ecological commitment, and appreciation of diversity).

It is the ideal place for the development of a "long memory" (Fernand Braudel).

— *Learning from the Mediterranean. Learning from Italy. Learning from Paris. Learning from Europe.* It is a pleasure to be able to paraphrase Robert Venturi and his *Learning from Las Vegas* (a study of symbolic architecture that has remained famed over the years and is particularly well-represented in the American gaming capital), but this time with the intention of using the text to evaluate AF517's propensity to produce a 'cultural' architecture that is never without context nor ever introduced as a UFO, but which, on the contrary, privileges a '*colta*' or 'cultivated' style. Alfonso Femia, both as an individual and a citizen, considers himself to be equally Italian and European.

We all know what Europe owes to Italy and, more widely, the Mediterranean since antiquity: a sense of statesmanship and collectiveness, a parallel concern for people, a spirit of inclusion, and a taste for interhuman exchanges and commerce.

Europe adds to this substrate with the modern era, its culture of enlightenment expressed through the attention paid to the universal rights represented by equality through birth, freedom

and the right to resistance when faced with oppression. Modernity, despite having often revealed itself to be overly expeditious, finally crowns this political edifice by injecting into this matrix legacy its taste for experimentation and experience, accepting the risk of adventure, as well as a visionary imperative based on a capacity to imagine.
To learn from the Mediterranean, Italy, Paris and Europe: in this school where the principal concepts combine depth and mobility, the education received by architects tends towards an educated vision. You don't throw out the baby or the bathwater. On the contrary, we deal with knowledge and points of view formulated within a framework of a situation deemed to be *complex*.
— A truthful architecture is never easy, nor will it ever be simplistic or a caricature of itself.
It implies having to question oneself insofar as this essential element is concerned: when it comes down to it, what exactly is the quintessence of architecture? The truth of the matter is that the quintessence of architecture is less than ever before reduced to a single formula that can simply be duplicated in the same way that one might reel off a mantra. AF517, or how to navigate a straight line without simply taking the shortest route.

— Architecture is inseparable from history which, in our consciences, is also the history of the future. History is rich and rather than impoverishing it, we should rub up against it by admitting the need to create in a complex universe. Rather than invent, we should federate visions, memories, expectations and dreams to enrich reality.

... the journey continues

BNP PARIBAS
SAMSUNG

OPEN
CARE
CAFE

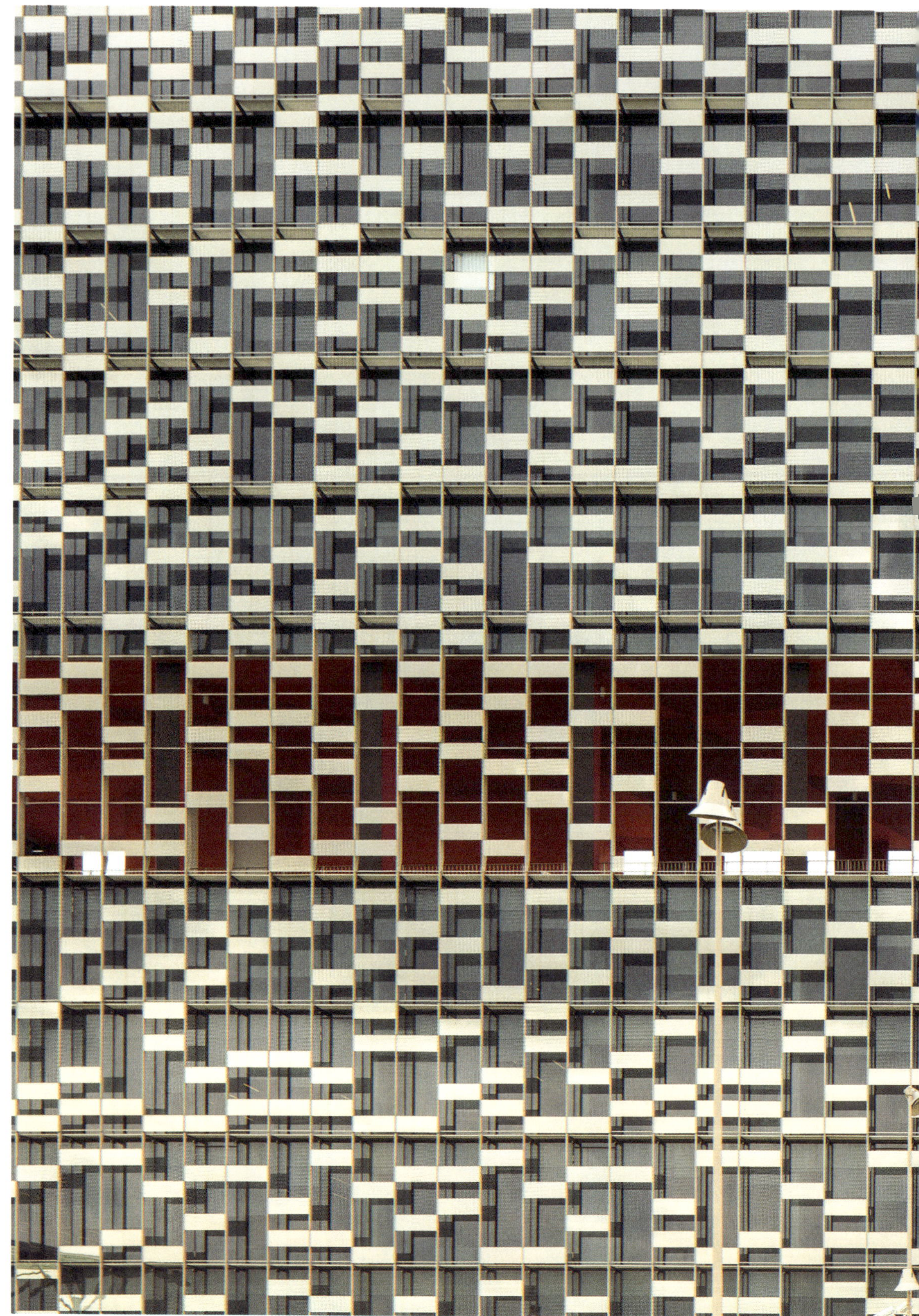

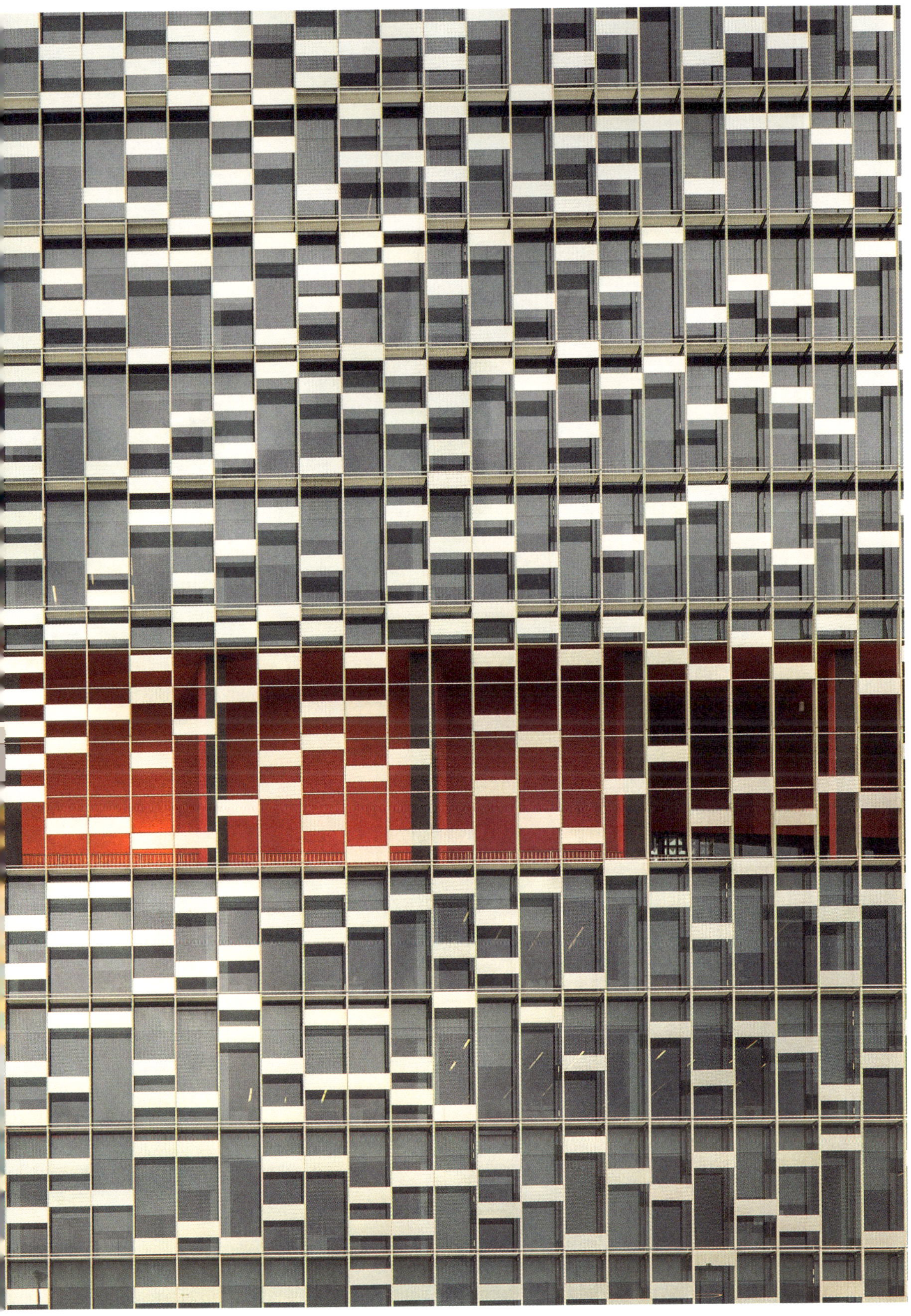

CRÉTEIL-L'ÉCHAT

BATTERIE TROMBE
FIAMM
Elettrauto

P

Roma Tiburtina

HORIZONTAL TOWER
Milan, Italy
2008 – 2010

THREE TOWERS
IN SAN BENIGNO
Genoa, Italy
2010 – 2015

THE CORNER
Milan, Italy
2014 – 2019

MUNICIPAL
LIBRARY
La Spezia, Italy
2012 – 2016

DALLARA ACADEMY
Varano de' Melegari, Italy
2015 – 2018

DALLARA ACADEMY
Varano de' Melegari, Italy
2015 – 2018

NEW BNL-BNP PARIBAS
HEADQUARTERS
Rome, Italy
2012 – 2017

IULM 6
UNIVERSITY
Milan, Italy
2003 – 2015

NEW VIMAR
LOGISTICS POLE
Marostica, Italy
2015 – ongoing

THE DOCKS
Marseille, France
2009 – 2015

THE DOCKS
Marseille, France
2009 – 2015

NEW BNL-BNP PARIBAS
HEADQUARTERS
Rome, Italy
2012 – 2017

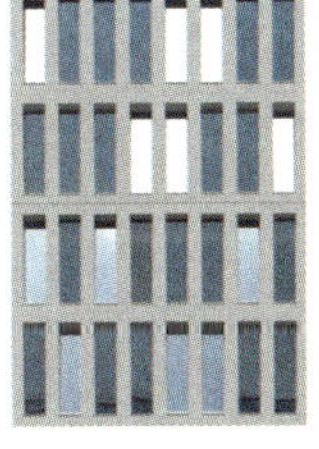

DALLARA ACADEMY
Varano de' Melegari, Italy
2015 – 2018

BÌ - TOY AND ARTS FACTORY
Cormano, Italy
2005 – 2010

PROGRAMMING AND URBAN STUDY
Bry, Champigny, France
2011

HORIZONTAL TOWER
Milan, Italy
2008 – 2010

THE GARDENS OF GABRIEL
Asnières-sur-Seine, France
2013 – 2016

SAN GIOVANNI EXHIBITION CENTRE
Casarza Ligure, Italy
2002 – 2008

EAI SITE
Montpellier, France
2018 – ongoing

THE CORNER
Milan, Italy
2014 – 2019

POSTE BRUNE
Paris XIV, France
2014 – 2017

THE CORNER
Milan, Italy
2014 – 2019

GREAT RAILWAYS WORKSHOPS
Turin, Italy
2009 – 2011

MC2 CREATIVITY CENTER
Marseilles, France
2018 – ongoing

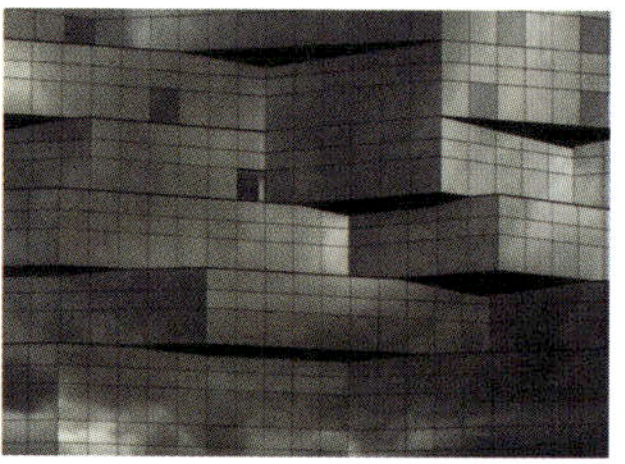

THE CORNER
Milan, Italy
2014 – 2019

NEW RESIDENTIAL DISTRICT
Brescia, Italy
2010 – 2013

EUROPACITY: AFFORDABLE HOTEL 3*
Gonesse, France
2017 – ongoing

NEW SCHOOL COMPLEX
Zugliano, Italy
2010 – 2013

DALLARA ACADEMY
Varano de' Melegari, Italy
2015 – 2018

HORIZONTAL TOWER
Milan, Italy
2008 – 2010

J1 THE ODYSSEY SUBAQUATIC CENTER
Marseille, France
2018

CONNECTED PROJECT OF GRAND PARIS EXPRESS
Créteil-l'Échat, France
2015 – ongoing

MILANESE ICE FACTORY
Milan, Italy
2002 – 2005

NEW BNL-BNP PARIBAS HEADQUARTERS
Rome, Italy
2012 – 2017

THE VAULTS OF ALGIERS
Algiers, Algeria
2018

THREE TOWERS IN SAN BENIGNO
Genoa, Italy
2010 – 2015

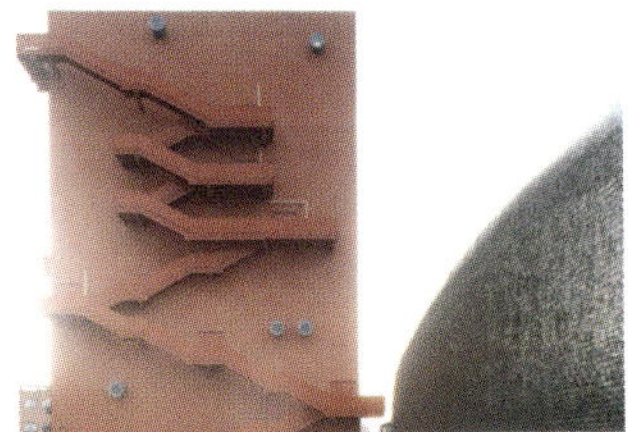

ITALIAN SPACE
AGENCY
Rome, Italy
2005 2012

THE GARDENS OF GABRIEL
Asnières-sur-Seine, France
2013 – 2016

TOURISTIC
COMPLEX
La Ciotat, France
2016 – ongoing

NEW BNL-BNP PARIBAS
HEADQUARTERS
Ceramic model
by Danilo Trogu

THE CORNER
Milan, Italy
2014 – 2019

NEW BNL-BNP PARIBAS
HEADQUARTERS
Rome, Italy
2012 – 2017

REDEVELOPMENT
1ST ITALIAN STATE MINT
Rome, Italy
2019 – ongoing

NEW CRUISE
TERMINAL
La Spezia, Italy
2019

IULM 6 UNIVERSITY
Milan, Italy
2003 – 2015

NEW BNL-BNP PARIBAS
HEADQUARTERS
Rome, Italy
2012 – 2017

REDEVELOPMENT
OF MARKET HALL
Aosta, Italy
2018

THE CORNER
Milan, Italy
2014 – 2019

Paul Ardenne

Paul Ardenne is Doctor of History and Science of Arts. As an art historian, writer and curator, he wrote several reference books on modern and contemporary creation: "Art, Contemporary Age" (1997), "Art in its Political Moment" (2000), "L'Image Corps" (2001), "A Contextual Art" (2002), "Art, the present" (2009), "Hundred artists of Street art" (2011), "Blessed are the creators?" (2016).
Latest books: "An ecological Art. Plastic and Anthropocene Creation" (essay, 2018) and "Roger-caught-in-the-Earth" (novel, 2017).

In the field of architecture, Paul Ardenne wrote several monographs (Rudy Ricciotti, FGP-a, Alain Sarfati, Jean-Paul Viguier, 5+1AA ...). "Human and urban globalization" (2005, 2nd edition 2010). He has been for ten years in the "Blockbuster" section of the journal "Archistorm", a detailed chronicle of the ultimate evolutions of architecture and urbanism.

Maurice Culot

Maurice Culot, an architect, town planner and publisher, is president of the European Arcas group, the Architecture Foundation in Brussels and the body awarding the Philippe Rotthier triennial European prize. In 1968, he founded AAM (Archives d'Architecture Modernes), a publishing house specialised in books on art and architecture. He is also the author and co-author of several books on Art Nouveau and Art Deco, including those concerning this heritage in Asnières-sur-Seine and Argenteuil.

The last two years have seen his growing interest in reminiscences concerning this movement in Paris through the publication of a number of books that include "Montparnasse 1900-1930 Art Nouveau-Art Déco", "Montparnasse du Rêve, Un art de vivre Art Déco" and "Montmartre 1900-1930 Art Nouveau-Art Déco". In March 2019, he received the American Richard H. Driehaus prize recognizing his lifetime commitment to the service of architecture and traditional town planning.

SCIANNA
VENICE
KM3
Sutter

Alfonso Femia

Alfonso Femia is the creator and co-founder of 5+1 agency in 1995, that became 5+1AA in 2005, and that is transformed into Atelier(s) Alfonso Femia in 2017.
In 2007, with the creation of the Parisian agency, Alfonso Femia develops the project themes in an 'atelier' gathering three places characteristic of the identity of the three cities, Genoa, Milan and Paris, where a multidisciplinary team makes them live like a unique place for project and thought, feeding on the different particularities and experiences of the three cities, the three geographies, the three stories. Alfonso Femia has been a Professor of Architectural Design Didactics at Kent State University in Florence, at the Universities of Ferrara and Genoa and visiting professor at the Hong-Kong University in China.
Since 1996, year of the "France 2013 - Italy 10" conference that he organised with 5+1 and M. Strata, Alfonso Femia has participated to numerous lectures about the use of architectural competitions as a project tool. From 1995 to 2000, together with Francesco Guerisoli, he has been the editorial advisor of Joshua Libri, which activity was the broadcasting of the architectural project and its contemporary representatives.
In 2015, he founds 500x100 with US Milan and creates 500x100Talk, a place of meetings and exchanges on the theme of the city, structured in two formats presented with the journalist Giorgio Tartaro: the SetTalk in Milan and the CityTalk in the main European and Mediterranean cities. In 2017, he has been chosen by the international magazine IQD to be Guest Editor and publishes a special issue on the "Invisible Mediterranean(s)", a theme with which he wants to affirm the centrality of the Mediterranean and the need to live a "slow time" in parallel with the speedness of our contemporaneity.
In 2018, he creates in Milan the "Maison 500x100" and "Regard(s)", a space dedicated to dialog, the confrontation with art, photography, literature, music, mankind.

In 2019, he has been nominated Editorial Advisor of the IQD magazine, where he develops the themes "Invisibile Brazil" – with Antoine Vernholes – and "Mediterranea" gathering a selection of international eyes and specific interviews.
He has received from the cultural association LP the medal of the Italian President of the Republic being the artistic director of the third edition of the Pisa Biennale, by developing the international call to action "Timeofwater, water as dimension of time."

The same year, he has been listed in the Aldi/Compasso d'Oro index with the project for the door handle "(IN)finito for DND Handle" and has been awarded by the German Design Awards 2020 for the "Drop by Drop" ceiling light produced by Guzzini.

Alfonso Femia has published several books over the years and the most recent are: "Les Docks Marseilles", "1 and 3 Towers", "The Entre-Deux" and "The Sky of Rome".

He loves odd numbers, the South and has been accompanied by a crew of women and men who, since 1995, have believed in this "journey" aimed to explore and experience the world through the architectural project and the meeting with the cities, all with a smile and new fellow travelers: "the whale and her star".

The journey inside the journey.

Atelier(s) Alfonso Femia

The Atelier(s) confront the contemporary in the way they address the relationship between territory, city and architecture, constructing this relationship as a representation of reality. A visionary pragmatism that feeds reality with its own imaginary and believes that the latter can get in touch with reality. The perception and the transformation of reality are the keys to a conception of architecture as both body and idea, at once real and emotional, pragmatic and sensual, acceptable and yet also capable of engendering wonder as a catalyst of new understanding. The research on matter, characteristic of the last projects made in Italy and France, is fundamental in the reassertion of matter as an empathic dimension of architecture when it encounters the ones who live it and occupy the city. Matter wants also generously reassert the importance of a close dialog between all the actors of the project, from the client to the craftsman. The Marseilles Docks are the reflection of the main themes developed by Atelier(s) AF517: the relation between public and private, the project as a place of destination. The dialog as a project tool and the project as a dialog tool are the actions that distinguish the thought of Atelier(s) Femia, believing in the project as an opportunity of encounters and exchanges; that is measured in and with time and that makes the chronotopic dimension one of the objectives of our research.

In 1995, when 5+1 was created, Alfonso Femia built the Forum of Aquileia, the University Campus of Savona, the Wyler Vetta Pavilion in Basel, the headquarters of the Ministry of the Interior in Rome, the Low Emission Building in Savona, the Ice Palace and the Ice Factory in Milan, the Assago Retail Park, the Villa Sottanis and the Exhibition Centre in Casarza Ligure, the Blend Building and the Blend Tower for General Properties in Milan, and the Marina Residence in Cotonou (with Peia Associates).

In 2005, 5+1AA was created and Alfonso Femia won the competition for the new Venice Cinema Palace with Rudy Ricciotti.

In 2006, he opened an Atelier in Milan, dedicated to the creation and the research on the contemporary city.
The same year, Simonetta Cenci became partner of 5+1AA and took the role of General Manager for the Ateliers of Genoa and Milan.

In 2007, he created 5+1AA in Paris, with the collaboration of Nicola Spinetto. The agency developed the masterplan that let Milan win the World Exposition 2015.

In 2008, he won the competition for the new Fiera Milan business headquarters, built in 2010 with Pietri Architectes.

In 2009, he won the competitions for the redevelopment of the Marseilles Docks for J.P. Morgan and Constructa Urban Systems and for the Great Railways Workshops in Turin, where the 150th anniversary celebrations of the Unification of Italy were held.

5+1AA

He also completes the reconstruction of a housing complex in San Giuliano di Puglia.

In 2010, he won the competition to design the Generali SGR residential complex in Milan and he also built the Toy and Arts Museum in Cormano.

In 2011, he won the Philippe Rotthier European Prize for Architecture in Brussels with the Ice Factory project in Milan and the International Chicago Athenaeum Award for the Horizontal Tower: new headquarters of the Fiera in Milan.

In 2012, he developed a program of housing in Évry, designed a strategic masterplan for the city of Palermo, a urban programming and study for the sector around the Grand Paris area, a masterplan for the Yeni Shenir in Istanbul and for the Secteur Étoile in Geneva.
He completed the building for the new Italian space agency in Rome. The same year, he won the competition for the new BNL-BNP Paribas headquarters in Rome and the competition for the urban requalification of the Michelet RRG site in Marseille with Carta Associés.
He won the Award Revealed Architectures with the Great Railways Workshops in Turin.

In 2013, he built the Deledda Centre, the requalification of the Beleno Barracks area in Venaria Reale and the new school complex in Zugliano. He won the competition for the regeneration of the former Fitram site in La Spezia, was entrusted with the reconversion of the Lots 4 and 9 of the harbour of Tangier and with a residential project of 183 housing units in Asnières-sur-Seine. He was invited to participate in international competitions in Algeria, Germany and China, where he was a finalist for the new cultural center of Yuangh with Marco Piva.

In 2014, he won the competition for the redevelopment of the Bank of Italy in Rome. He participated at the competition for the project of the new tramway in Istanbul and was invited for the new Ferragamo logistics center in Florence.

In 2015, he completed the Marseille Docks, the university building IULM 6 in Milan and the GLF/MSC Cruises towers in Genoa.
He won the competition for the construction of a student residence, a hotel and offices in Créteil-l'Échat with MG-AU and the one for the Dallara Academy: the construction of a training and exhibition centre in Varano de' Melegari, Parma.

In 2016, he completed the projects of the new headquarters of BNL-BNP Paribas in Rome, the residential complex gathering 183 housing units in Asnières-sur-Seine, the interior arrangement of Groupe La Poste headquarters in Paris and the redevelopment of Cantore former barracks into a music school in Cuneo.
The Marseille Docks were rewarded in several national and international awards including the MIPIM Awards in Cannes, the LEAF Awards in London, the ULI "Global Awards For Excellence" in Dallas and The Plan Awards. The Plan International Awards also rewarded the project of the new BNL-BNP Paribas headquarters in Rome, also finalist in other awards including the Mipim Awards 2017, as the Gardens of Gabriel in Asnières-sur-Seine.

In 2017, the residential complex in Asnières-sur-Seine and the Dallara Academy were rewarded with a special mention in the The Plan Awards. The latter also won the LEAF Awards in London as best "project under construction". The projects of the Marseille Docks, the university building IULM 6 in Milan and the LIFE residential complex in Brescia won the first Prize of the Ceramic and the Project.

In 2018, the Atelier(s) Alfonso Femia won the competitions for the 3* Affordable Chic Hotel in Europacity, the transformation of the former Infantry School into housing in Montpellier and the redevelopment of two universities in Marseille and Avignon.

In 2019, the Atelier(s) Alfonso Femia won the international competition for the redevelopment and recovery of the complex of the first Italian state mint in Rome and the construction of offices in Toulouse-Blagnac airport area for the project "Dessine-moi Toulouse".
The Atelier(s) Alfonso Femia ended the project "The Corner", a redevelopment of offices building in Milan, rewarded, as the Dallara Academy, at The Plan Awards 2019.

The Dallara Academy and the project of the Gardens of Gabriel in Asnières-sur-Seine have also been rewarded at the international Grand Prix Casalgrande Padana.

ATELIERFEMIA.COM
alfonsofemiadesign.com
insidethewhaleaf517.com

themooncodex727.com
cubomagico240.com
500x100.com

entre-deux.500x100.com
mediterraneiinvisibili.com
tempodacqua.com

Alfonso Femia
founding architect
partner and President

Simonetta Cenci
associate architect
deputy Managing Director

Sara Gottardo
associate architect
director of Paris Atelier

Alessandro Bellus
director of Milan Atelier
engineering, architecture

Marco Corazza
director of Milan Atelier
architecture

Sara Traverso
project director for
France Atelier Genoa

Amandine Aubrée
Stefania Bracco
Luca Bonsignorio
Fabio Marchiori
Valentin Mazet
Marcello Morino
Carola Picasso
Raffaella Francesca Pirrello
Alessandra Quarello
Francesca Recagno
project managers Atelier(s)

Sara Massa
project and computer-generated
imagery director Atelier(s)

Enrico Martino
project, design and graphics
director Atelier(s)

Roxana Calugar
Angela Cavallari
Arianna Dall'Occa
Stefano Delogu
Alfonso Marotta
Vittoria Paternostro
Giacomo Quercia
Maria Michela Scala
Vincenzo Tripodi
Carlotta Turrato
architects Atelier(s)

Stefano Cioncoloni
Carlo Occhipinti
computer-generated imagery
managers Genoa Atelier

Luca Aly
Lorenza Barabino
Simone Giglio
Carla Pugliese
BIM Managers Atelier(s)

Joanna Adracta
Elisabetta Alfonsi
Enrico Baudoin
Carolina Bustos
Federico Demoro
Carlo Consalvo
Giovanni De Grandi
Alessio Granada
Mehdi Reddaa
Rodolfo Siccardi
collaborators Atelier(s)

Liloye Chevallereau
director of research and
development, communication
Paris

Gianmatteo Ferlin
Natalee Christine Rojo
communication, press,
social media, web

Margherita Venturi
invitations to tender administrative
manager Atelier(s)

Romana Mazzarello
Antonella Muzzi
Agathe Christien
administration Atelier(s)

Francesca Mollura
secretary

Sergio Tani
IT, multimedia and web manager

"The air around suddenly vibrated and tingled, as it were, like the air over intensely heated plates of iron. Beneath this atmospheric waving and curling, and partially beneath a thin layer of water, also, the whales were swimming. Seen in advance of all the other indications, the puffs of vapour they spouted, seemed their forerunning couriers and detached flying outriders."

Herman Melville
"Moby Dick", 1851

Alfonso Femia and Simonetta Cenci would like to thank Luciana Ravanel for this new voyage 'inside the whale' carried out with passion and devotion, as well as all members of the Ante Prima Consultants team for their tireless work, Maurice Culot and AAM that, for many years, have worked alongside Alfonso Femia and the Atelier(s) in the development of their ideas, Rossella Martignoni and Marsilio Editori, for their analysis, dialogue and the generous amount of time they have provided, Gianluigi Pescolderung, «maestro» and friend who ensured that we were always able to look beyond the horizon, the Atelier(s) teams, an inseparable, unique and magical group of comrades who have battled shoulder to shoulder and lived through some unforgettable moments.

Alfonso Femia would particularly like to thank his closest friends, the managers of the Atelier(s) who have all been fully committed to this journey and the vision represented by AF517, as well as Simonetta, a professional partner who has also accompanied our challenges and dreams.

Particular thanks to my family and to my mother for all the values she has taught me, with her eyes and her smile, with her courage and sincerity.

Thanks to Paul Ardenne for the time spent between his trips to Italy and his moments in Paris, and for the authenticity of his presentation.

Thanks to the artist Danilo Trogu for all his comings and goings and his ongoing dialogue between art and architecture achieved through his ceramics that have proven able to illustrate the project's imaginative aspects.

Thanks to all the contractors who provided their trust and support and share their enthusiasm in travelling with us.

Thanks to all the craftsmen and women, masons, companies and industrialists who, with willingness and generosity, developed a research approach to their projects that included an understanding of the need for dialogue and a willingness to escape the «catalogue» of contemporary mediocrity.

Thanks also to our photographer friends who allowed us to depict our imaginary realism.

publishing house
Marsilio Editori
Santa Marta, Fabbricato
Demaniale, 17
30123 Venezia, Italia

production
Ante Prima Consultants
58, rue Beaubourg
75003 Paris, France

publication manager
Luciana Ravanel | Ante Prima

coordination and editorial work
Gianmatteo Ferlin |
Atelier(s) Alfonso Femia

authors
Paul Ardenne
Maurice Culot

editorial project
and artistic direction
Gianluigi Pescolderung,
Marta Vianello | studio Tapiro
Alfonso Femia, Simonetta Cenci,
Enrico Martino | AF*design

graphic design and preparation of drawings and images
studio Tapiro
with
AF*design
Gianmatteo Ferlin
Natalee Christine Rojo
Enrico Martino

translations
Nick Hargreaves

photographs
© Stefano Anzini (pp. 14, 15, 16, 17, 18, 19 , 20, 21, 24, 25, 31, 32, 36, 37, 40, 41, 46, 47, 56, 57, 110-113, 136-137, 156-157, 164, 167)
© Filippo Avandero (pp. 170-171)
© Luc Boegly (pp. 22, 23, 26, 27, 28, 29, 32, 33, 34, 35, 37, 38, 39, 116-121, 132-135, 140-145)
© Ernesta Caviola (pp. 2, 12, 13, 42, 43, 44, 45, 52, 53, 54, 55, 114-115, 128-129, 138-139, 152-153)
© Clément Guillaume (p. 168)

renderings
© AF517 (pp. 48, 49, 50, 51, 58, 122-127, 130-131, 146-151, 154-155)

ceramic model
© Danilo Trogu – La casa dell'Arte di Albisola (pp. 152-153)

printing
Ingoprint, Barcelona
www.ingoprint.com

© 2019 / Atelier(s) Alfonso Femia |
Marsilio Editori
ISBN: 978-88-297-0417-0

Available through
ARTBOOK | D.A.P.
75 Broad Street, Suite 630
New York, NY 10004
www.artbook.com

www.atelierfemia.com
www.marsilioeditori.it
www.ante-prima.com

All rights reserved. All information published in this book (drawings, photos, texts) are protected by intellectual property rights. No part of this publication may be reproduced, modified, translated, transmitted in any form or by any means, without the prior written permission of the publisher.

© Cédric Dasaesson